15.95

Gerrilyn Smith has a degree in Psychology and English Literature. She moved to London in 1976, where she obtained an M.Phil. in Clinical Psychology. She has worked in a number of settings, including voluntary agencies, the health service, local authority and private sector provision – all focusing on child protection services. She ran the Department of Health Postgraduate Training programme in Child Sexual Abuse which aimed to develop assessment and treatment services for children and families where sexual abuse was an issue. She has lectured and published widely in the field. She co-authored (with Kathy Nairne) the bestselling *Dealing with Depression* (The Women's Press, 1984, and fully revised and updated, with new material, 1995). Gerrilyn Smith currently works as a freelance trainer, consultant and clinician.

D1411618

S

Also by Gerrilyn Smith from The Women's Press:

With Kathy Nairne *Dealing with Depression* (1984, and fully revised and updated, with new material, 1995)

GERRILYN SMITH

the
Protectors'
Handbook

Reducing the risk of child sexual abuse
and helping children recover

First published by The Women's Press Ltd, 1995
A member of the Namara Group
34 Great Sutton Street, London EC1V 0DX

British Library Cataloguing-in-Publication Data
A catalogue record for this book is available from the British Library

ISBN 0 7043 4417 3

Phototypeset by Intype, London
Printed and bound in Great Britain by
BPC Paperbacks Ltd
A member of
The British Printing Company Ltd

To my sun and our rain with love

Acknowledgements

This book has been a long time coming through a whole series of events both personal and professional; some avoidable, others completely unavoidable, so thanks are due to a great many individuals who have helped bring this project to an end. To Hannah Kanter, my original editor, who started this off by urging me to write this book, and giving me her professional backing to do so; to Kathy Gale, my current editor, who took on the project and who has managed to suggest alterations while at the same time encouraging me to carry on; to all the children and mothers who have worked with me sharing their painful experiences and struggles to recover, but especially Natasha, Alison and Lisa who agreed to be interviewed for this book; to Tina, Kim, Marcia, Moire and Marie who agreed to be critical readers of the first draft and gave me permission to use some of their feedback in the book; and finally to Jennifer Peck who rescued me at the end when I thought I couldn't go on any more, by preparing the manuscript and who helped organise the resources. My thanks and gratitude to you all – in your own way you have all been inspirational.

Contents

Section One: Reducing Risk

Chapter One   1

Introduction to and Outline of this Book   1
General Characteristics of Sexual Abuse   4
How to Protect Children   6

Chapter Two   9

Recognising Signs and Indicators   9
   Under-fives age group   11
   Five to twelve age group   21
   Twelve to sixteen age group   30
Following up Your Concerns   36

Chapter Three   38

Reducing the Risks and Helping Children to Tell   38
   'Keeping safe'   39
   Body awareness   39
   Knowing your child's social network and surroundings   40
   Types of touching   41
   Secrets   42
   Encouraging children to tell   42
   Rehearsal   43
   Using books and other resources   43
Following up Concerns   44
What to Do if a Child Chooses You to Tell   49
Protecting the Child Immediately After a Disclosure   51

Section Two: Facilitating Recovery

Chapter Four   57

Establishing a Context for Recovery   57
   What the child needs   58
   Your belief   58
   Your understanding   60

Being clear about who is responsible   61
What you need   62
Give yourself time and space   62
Getting support for yourself   63
Talking about it with family   65
Involving friends and community   67
Blocks to being an effective protector   68
Not believing   68
Vulnerabilities   69
Survivors and parenting   70
Ongoing abuse   71
Maintaining the Context for Recovery   72

Chapter Five   74

The Emotional Consequences of Sexual Abuse   74
  Areas of concern   77
  *Developing an appropriate body image and healthy
self-esteem*   77
  Developing a positive self-image   79
  Learning to have and express feelings appropriately 81
  Judging safe people and situations   83
  Developing an appropriate sense of responsibility   84
  Developing an understanding about right and wrong   86
  Developing positive relationships   88
  Developing a positive sexual identity   89
  Developing good communication skills   92
  Developing appropriate personal authority issues   94
Dealing with the Consequences   95

Chapter Six   98

The Healing Process   98
  Getting professional help   102
  Expertise in and approach to sexual abuse work   104
  Confidentiality   105
  Feedback   106
  Availability between sessions   106
  Timescale   107
  Expectations   107
  Criteria for termination   109
  Evaluation of change   110
  Other treatment issues   111
  Goals of treatment work   113

Different types of work to help children heal 114
Family work 114
Group work 115
Individual work 117
Managing challenging behaviours 118

Chapter Seven 122

Using the Statutory Agencies 122
Reporting Abuse 122
The Child Protection Committee 123
Case conferences and the Child Protection Register 123
Investigative interview 126
Medical examinations 128
Legal proceedings 130
Criminal proceedings 131
Press coverage 135
Civil proceedings 136
Criminal Injuries Compensation 142

Afterword 148

Appendix 158
Resources and Useful Addresses 158

Notes and References 185

Different types of work to help children deal 174
Family work 114
Group work 133
Therapeutic work ....
Sharing difficult situations 118

Chapter Nine

Using the Structure Diagram ....
Contraindications ....
The Child Protection Committee ....
Other issues in applying Child Protection Structure ....
Emotions burden ....
Making conclusions ....
Legal boundaries ....
Criminal proceedings ....
Data accuracy ....
Confidence changes ....
Constructing the Cooperation ....

Afterword 158

Appendix
Resources and Useful Addresses 168

Notes and References 195

A note on using the book

The table of contents is designed to give you a clear idea of what is contained in each chapter.

Within each chapter, any name in bold print indicates that the address is listed in the appendix.

Resources are also listed, grouped together by topic and target age range and connected to chapters in the book.

Notes and references for each chapter can be found at the end of the book.

CHAPTER ONE

Introduction to and Outline of this Book

In the last decade there has been an increasing awareness of sexual abuse of children and its long-term consequences. This has resulted in a number of services focusing specifically on child protection for children growing up now, as well as providing resources for those who were sexually abused as children but as adults are still struggling with the after-effects.

Despite this growing awareness that sexual abuse does happen, there is still much controversy about the scale of the problem. The most recent figures available on the prevalence of sexual abuse suggest that 47 per cent of the population will experience some form of unwanted sexually intrusive episode before 18 years of age; with 1 per cent experiencing sexual abuse by a father or father figure.[1]

There has also been much publicity regarding what is termed False Memory Syndrome, where people recover memories of sexual abuse that they previously repressed and which are considered to be untrue by others – usually the alleged perpetrators. It is unfortunate that the issue of false memories should receive so much public attention, since this detracts from the struggle that survivors, supporting protectors and professional child protection workers have mounted to get sexual abuse recognised in the first place.

The existence of sexual abuse in childhood cannot be denied. Child protection workers and those professionals involved in working with sex offenders know from their experience that the problem is widespread and that considerable resources will be needed for the foreseeable future both to protect children from future sexual abuse and to help all those – adults and children, perpetrators and victims – to recover from the devastating consequences. In recent research on adult mental health, as many as 50 per cent of women and

20 per cent of men receiving psychiatric treatments were found to have a history of sexual abuse in their childhoods.[2] While most adults are not abusers, to be non-abusing when sexual abuse is so widespread and its consequences so disturbing is not enough. We must all play an active role in reducing the risk of child sexual abuse happening in the first place.

Surrounding any child in the community is a network of adults. Within this network are both possible protectors and perpetrators, with the former outnumbering the latter. Yet possible protectors are frequently not able to prevent sexual abuse, nor able to promote recovery from the experience for any one child because rather than acting as protectors, they function as non-abusing adults. This book aims to transform non-abusing adults into protectors by providing information regarding sexual abuse that will help to reduce the risk of sexual abuse occurring and aid the recovery of those who have already experienced it.

This book provides a practical guide to effective protection and to helping children recover from an experience of sexual abuse. It is a book for all adults who want resources and information so they can feel more confident in identifying and raising the issue of sexual abuse in their families and their communities. It is also, but by no means exclusively, intended to be useful to professional child protection workers.

The first section of the book concentrates on ways to reduce the risk of child sexual abuse. It includes advice on talking to children before sexual abuse happens. This is based on the belief that it will be easier for children to tell adults about inappropriate or uncomfortable contact if there has been previous discussion about it. If you are used to talking to your child or to children close to you about difficult issues, you will have a base on which to build the trust and empathy that are necessary for the child's recovery process, should sexual abuse occur. This part of the book gives clear advice on the signs and indicators that might suggest child sexual abuse and discusses in detail how to decide whether sexual abuse is the most likely explanation for what you have observed or been told. There follows clear guidance about what you can do if a child you know tells you about being sexually abused; or if you feel that the signs and indicators do suggest sexual abuse.

The second section of the book concentrates on the recovery process. The emotional consequences of a child being sexually abused are described, including some of the more challenging behaviours that the child may display. Suggestions are made about how to deal with challenging behaviours. Establishing a good context for recovery is extremely important for any child trying to deal with an experience of sexual abuse. There is clear advice about what constitutes a good context for recovery and how you can help to establish it. You may need to use statutory agencies and legal proceedings, which can be complicated and sometimes frightening. This part of the book includes a full description of the statutory agencies and advice on how to get the best from them. There is a resource list which includes a wide range of books and videos for both adults and children. Some helpful addresses are also included.

This book comes from my experience as a child psychologist working in the field of child protection. I have worked in many different contexts including a telephone counselling line, a local child mental health clinic, a Social Services department, a teaching hospital and, most recently, a girls' residential unit. It is also firmly based on the experiences of survivors of sexual abuse, both adults and children, who agreed to help me with this book. Their names and some identifying details have been changed in order to protect their confidentiality.

For various reasons, the agencies which currently exist to deal with child sexual abuse cannot be wholly effective in reducing the risk of sexual abuse or helping the child and possible protectors when sexual abuse becomes apparent. Most resources focus on the apprehension of offenders, with an inordinate amount of professional time going into investigations that never get anywhere near criminal courts. For example, in one area within one London borough over the period 1990–92, there were a total of 1,476 referrals for joint police and social work investigation. Of those, 590 (40 per cent) were referrals for sexual abuse. Criminal charges were brought in 91 cases, 15 per cent of the total number of referrals for sexual abuse. Of that proportion, only six convictions were secured, three of which did not involve a prison sentence.[3]

One recent study of children's perceptions of the professional response to sexual abuse identified 202 children who were all considered to have been sexually abused by the professionals working with them. Of those cases only one in three resulted in criminal prosecutions bring brought, and only one in four perpetrators were convicted.[4] This represents an enormous amount of professional time and effort going into the investigative process, producing a very small return in terms of the number of criminal convictions secured.

But before even reaching the stage of a formal investigation, someone has to recognise that sexual abuse may be happening. If the child has told someone, they will have to be believed and the adults surrounding that child will need to secure the child's protection from any further sexual abuse. The criminal justice system alone does not fulfil these functions. It is therefore essential that the adults surrounding children in their day-to-day lives are able to talk about the issues of sexual abuse, recognise the indicators that suggest it may be happening, and feel powerful and informed enough to act on the child's behalf.

General Characteristics of Sexual Abuse

Defining sexual abuse can be difficult, even if you have experienced it yourself. The desire to deny it has happened or to minimise its effects is often overwhelming for all concerned. Even with a lot of help and guidance, it can still be difficult to identify and articulate. However, there are some general characteristics of sexual abuse that are well documented, and repeated in study after study.

The vast majority of sexual assaults on children are committed by people known to the child.[5] Assaults by strangers clearly happen but they are the minority of cases. They also do not carry the same reporting restrictions, so consequently we hear more about them in the media. The single largest category of offenders is fathers and father figures (this includes step-fathers, foster or adoptive fathers, male cohabitees, mother's boyfriend). There is also increasing evidence of a large amount of unwanted sexual contact from other juveniles, especially brothers.[6]

Sexual abuse can start at any age. It rarely involves one episode of sexual abuse but more often involves many episodes, and many acts. The age it starts at can be difficult to identify as it often begins with appropriate touching which gradually becomes inappropriate. Sexual offenders purposely disguise sexual touching to be confusing both to the child who experiences it and, perhaps more importantly, to anyone who inadvertently observes it. With very young children, it often occurs around bathtime, during toileting or nappy changes, and at bedtimes, where a benign cover of appropriate touching can confuse any possible protectors. Many children will date the start of their abuse from the point at which penetration is attempted. However, it would be safe to assume that by this time there has been other, more ambiguous touching that has occurred as part of the softening-up or grooming process.

Force, whilst always implicit in child sexual abuse, is rarely used. The role of violence is more evident when the perpetrator is not known to the victim. In the majority of cases, where perpetrators know their targets, powerful threats and sometimes bribes ensure co-operation. The close proximity and the ongoing relationship between perpetrator and abused child mean that the threats can be reinforced periodically, the target can be reminded by the perpetrator of the consequences that disclosure will bring, and bribes can be used that may be especially tantalising to a particular child.

Sexual abuse is a premeditated crime. The individual who commits it has thought about it and planned how to do it.

(Even in attacks by strangers, where the target is randomly chosen, it is still planned and premeditated.)

> He'd, like, bring me out and be all nice, but I always knew it was going to happen at the end, he'd like be all nice and buy me everything that I wanted, you know, and in the end just do it all over again.
>
> He used to come up to the school to pick me up – like, my mum would be up there, my sister, but he wouldn't bring them two home, he'd just give me a lift home, you know – he would always take me out, he wouldn't take the rest of them out.
>
> All the things he bought me and did for me, it was like I owed him something.
>
> (Alison)

Many people feel more comfortable believing that sexual abuse is a momentary, impulsive lapse of self-control. But the reality is quite different.

How to Protect Children

Much work has been done to try and identify factors that contribute to an episode of sexual abuse. David Finkelhor has identified four factors that are critical in any episode of sexual abuse.[7] They are: (1) the presence of an individual with a motivation to sexually abuse children who (2) overcomes their own internal inhibitors against such behaviour and (3) the protectors surrounding the child and (4) the child's own resistance.

Effective intervention needs to be directed at each of these identified factors both before possible sexual abuse happens and to help those who have already experienced sexual abuse. Such intervention should include treatment resources for sex offenders, the children who have been sexually abused and the adults, often primary caregivers who are trying to help the child recover and who frequently need help themselves in coming to terms with what has happened.

Teaching children to be assertive, to say no and get away (addressing Finkelhor's fourth factor above) does not adequately deal with the subtlety and complexity of sexual abuse by known, often trusted adult caregivers. The bulk of the protective task should rest with adults, with children taking only a developmentally appropriate level of responsibility for protecting themselves.

There is much debate about whether convicting sexual offenders is the best form of protection in the longer term. This could partially address Finkelhor's factor one, by removing potential perpetrators, but there are many convincing arguments to suggest that, in and of itself, conviction of sexual offenders is not enough to protect children in the future.

As we have seen, most sexual abusers are not convicted. When they are, many are not given a custodial sentence, others serve relatively short sentences. Very few receive any psychological help to stop them from reoffending. Whilst they may return to families who know about the sexual abuse, many will move on to new families where knowledge regarding their past sexually offending behaviour is not available or fully understood.

> He's gonna do it again – if he gets away with it he's gonna do it again. People like him don't stop. And now that he's got away with it once, he's gonna think he can get away with it again . . . he's got children – he's probably doing it to them.
>
> (Alison)

In addition, research suggests that custodial sentences, far from preventing further sexually offending behaviour, can increase it.[8] There is evidence to suggest that some sexual offenders are organised, and organising together to share ideas, strategies to avoid detection, helpful hints on how to sexually offend, and are swapping or sharing their victims.[9]

It is likely that time in prison gives a sexual offender an opportunity to network with others who have a similar interest in sexual abuse.

So, increasing the effectiveness of all the possible external inhibitors to sexual abuse has to be an integral part of protecting children. Children need to be surrounded by a community of adults amongst whom the majority are possible protectors.[10] Sexual abusers are often very skilled at rearranging the child's network so that they are closer to the child than any possible protectors. It is therefore crucial that possible protecting adults have all the skills and information necessary to recognise the signs of sexual abuse, and to know what to do if it occurs.

Many people, including some professionals, still believe that children lie about sexual abuse or make up allegations; that only strangers sexually molest children; that it only happens once; that mothers always know if it is happening; that it is easy to prevent or stop; that only certain types of people sexually abuse children; that it only happens in certain communities or certain families; that it isn't so bad really; that if children didn't like it they would tell. But like it or not, sexual abuse is commonplace and will touch all of us, either personally through our families and communities or professionally in our work, especially if we work with children.

Non-abusing as a stance is no longer good enough. As adults, we must move from a passive, non-abusing stance to a more proactive, protecting stance, in order to protect our children.

CHAPTER TWO

Recognising Signs and Indicators

This chapter examines some of the indicators that suggest child sexual abuse may be happening. Clearly this is important information for primary caregivers of children and young people. This includes parents, grandparents and other relatives as well as teachers, nursery nurses, foster caregivers, residential workers, health visitors, general practitioners – virtually anyone who comes into contact with children and young people.

Adults should know about these indicators because expecting children to verbally articulate what is happening to them when they are being sexually abused places too large a responsibility on the child to tell.

> He used to say to me that if I ever told, my mum would hate me and she'd – you know – do this and do that. And it was also embarrassment, and you blame yourself – you're thinking 'I should have said no, I should have done this' to have stopped him. So I thought that I'd get the blame if I told . . .
>
> (Alison)

There are many valid and compelling reasons not to tell. The fear of being disbelieved is one of the most common.

> I couldn't tell Mum – I felt I was letting her down . . . 'cause after what he had told me, I didn't know what to expect from her; I thought she wouldn't believe me . . . it sounded too unbelievable . . . she might turn round and say 'Why would he be doing it to you?'
>
> (Alison)

Adults in contact with children must have the courage to guess, or at least to be curious, when children show signs that they are confused or worried about something.

> It's easier if someone else says it, rather than coming out with it, like – you know – someone's touching you.
>
> (Alison)

> Karen [social worker] sort of guessed something was going on, and like, she helped me bring it out in the open. I think, like, she, like, was picking up hints and everything, and, like, she was trying to piece them together and then she just came up with this and asked me and through the tears and everything I finally said yes.
>
> (Natasha)

But it is also important to know that not all children are worried by sexual abuse. This may be because they are very young and do not understand that it is wrong; or because in their family, it is the norm; or because they have no experience of it not happening.

> I think it really took a lot for, like, me to, like, think 'This is wrong, this is not supposed to happen . . .', 'cause they were family and – you look up to them and think of them as an example. It really takes a lot to, like, understand that they do it, and they're not supposed to, and they know they're not supposed to.
>
> (Natasha)

There are some behavioural signs that are very suggestive of sexual abuse. In the table at the end of this chapter, there is a list of such signs and indicators arranged by age. This list should be used as a guide only. It is most likely that if sexual abuse is happening there will be a number of signs and indicators from all of the categories that have been present for quite some time. The categories are arranged into red alert to indicate high risk, green for moderate risk and blue to indicate low risk.

When assessing indicators of sexual abuse, it is important to take into account the child's current development. What may be appropriate behaviour for an older child, may indicate a problem for a younger child or vice versa.

The following discussion regarding the indicators is divided into different age ranges, focusing primarily on the red alert signs for each group.

Remember that regardless of the number of indicators, it is still important to fully investigate any concerns you have and to be prepared to have them either confirmed or disconfirmed by gathering more information.

Under-fives age group

This age range clearly represents the pre-school child. There are some characteristics of this age range that will help possible protectors be more alert to the indicators of sexual abuse, and this is especially important because a significant proportion of this age range have little or no language. One of those indicators will be physical signs. However, many types of sexual abuse will not leave any physical indicator. If you notice any injuries to a child's genitals these should be investigated immediately. Many mothers of babies who have been sexually abused notice differences in the child's genitals or anus, and sometimes this will be pointed out to health visitors, GPs or nursery staff. These kinds of concerns should always be taken seriously and investigated further by a paediatrician with knowledge of sexual abuse and who is prepared, if necessary, to be involved in court proceedings. No parent wants their child to be medically examined more than is necessary. It is therefore important that the right professional does the examination. Otherwise the wrong opinion regarding risk can be given, important medical evidence may be lost, and the appropriate medical follow-up may not be made (such as testing for venereal diseases).

Despite limited verbal ability, children in this age range

often do tell adults about being sexually abused. Because their disclosures are so brief, often containing only the essential elements of who did what, many adults do not take them seriously or give them credence. In this age range children tend to be naïve disclosers. They are too young to know the consequences of disclosing and often do not really understand the true meaning of secrets. If they were asked to tell you what they were told not to tell you, it is likely they would oblige.

Spontaneous disclosures in this age range frequently occur in a context where one would least expect them. They contain essential detail but little elaboration, and the child often does not realise the significance of what they have said. For example, one nursery worker was asking her group of ten two-to-three-year-olds what they did before they came to nursery in the morning. One little girl, Evelyn, said very clearly, 'Daddy fuck my bum.' The nursery worker, who was quite shocked by the child's utterance, said 'Pardon?' and the child repeated what she had originally said.

In a significant number of cases in this age range the child will show a range of behavioural disturbances that will be noticed by primary caregivers. One of the largest single categories of these disturbances is sexualised behaviour. Masturbatory behaviour is one example. Many children in this age range do masturbate without this being an indication of sexual abuse. It becomes a red alert sign when it has a compulsive quality to it: the child does it in preference to other activities; normal tactics of dissuasion are unsuccessful in getting the child interested in something else; and it occurs in a range of different contexts, not just, for instance, prior to going to sleep. It can also involve putting objects into either the vagina, the penis or the anus.

By the time the child has reached the age of five, most primary caregivers will have helped their child to learn the social etiquette of masturbatory behaviour. The child may have received strong inhibitory messages about doing it at all. Most will have been encouraged to do it privately in safe places like their bedroom. Masturbation is a perfectly normal behaviour and should not cause alarm in parents. It can be compared to other behaviours which are antisocial in public, such as nose-picking, which again most parents manage to steer children towards doing less conspicuously and in approved places.

When masturbatory behaviour has qualities which make it a concern, it is important that primary caregivers make an effort to discover why this has become a preoccupation with the child. Clearly in a child with no language this is problematic. However it can be a signal that someone, and most usually an adult, has made the child's genitals a focus of attention. Children can experience sexual arousal if their genitals are stimulated and an adult who knows this can exploit the physical dependence of the small child. Compulsive masturbatory behaviour would not arise from accidental contact with a caregiver.

Often compulsive masturbatory behaviour is accompanied by anxiety, other signs of distress, or hyperarousal. It is important that if this is the case adults who care for the child notice the behaviour and report it. In Evelyn's case, the nursery staff had observed her masturbating in the nursery. She was not private about it and the behaviour was accompanied by loud grunts and groans from the child that sounded quite strange and unchildlike. This child also had a fear of having her nappy changed and would scream to keep it on.

Compulsive masturbatory behaviour is a red alert sign of abuse. Other behaviours that fall within the red alert section of the list include sexualised drawings, developmentally inappropriate sexual knowledge, and overt sexual approaches to other children and adults.

Primary caregivers of children in this age range will have seen many drawings. If children draw people and mark in their genitals it is important to be curious as to why this part of the body is receiving such attention at this time. For example, a young boy started drawing all of his people with breasts following the birth of a sibling. His mother was breastfeeding and breasts became significant enough to mark on his drawings. After a while he stopped. Clearly this is not a case of sexual abuse and indeed the little boy had no other signs or indicators of sexual abuse.

Heston and Norleen – two children involved in an access case where their mother was worried that their father had sexually abused them – began their interview with investigators by drawing pictures of themselves. They both drew large circles for people with arms and legs coming from the circle. Eyes, nose and mouth were carefully marked in, and then in between the legs they both noted 'ting-a-lings'. This spontaneous introduction of genitals in their drawings needed to be followed up.

Primary caregivers often have a good intuitive understanding of what constitutes developmentally appropriate sexual knowledge. You will probably know what your child knows about the 'facts of life' because it is most likely that you will have told them yourself. Children begin by asking questions about where babies come from. The mechanics of how the baby 'got in' and how the baby 'got out' will come later. Children in this age range are preoccupied with excretion and how their private parts work in relation to weeing and pooing, since toilet training occurs in this age range. Some children will have discovered pleasurable feelings from touching their genitals. However specific knowledge regarding sexual acts, in particular knowledge of penetration and/or oral sex, is extremely unusual in this age range.

Primary caregivers should be able to identify where sexual knowledge has come from. It is unlikely to come from accidentally viewing a pornographic film (one common explanation), or accidentally walking into their parents' bedroom and seeing them involved in sexual activity. A one-off accidental view like this is unlikely to produce the kind of inappropriate sexual behaviour described in this section. Inappropriate sexual knowledge manifests itself as a preoccupation by the child; something they talk about and make reference to constantly – often something they are trying to understand. If a parent has elected to give an under-five-year-old sex education, it is unlikely that it would lead to behavioural disturbances. If the sex lessons came with demonstrations, this would constitute sexual abuse. It is for children to discover how their bodies work for themselves, not for adults to show them.

Direct, often explicit, sexual overtures are a red alert indicator. Children in this age range do not know that sexual contact between adult and child is wrong, and if a child has been initiated into sexual behaviour they may try to engage others in such activities. For example, these extracts from a foster mother's diary demonstrate clearly not only overt sexual overtures but also the four-year-old child's sexual preoccupations.

7 January 1990
Martin tried to lick my genitals through my clothes whilst sitting on the floor between my legs. Martin says that he does this to Mummy and Daddy . . .

14 January 1990
Martin showed me his penis. When I said why did I want to see that, he replied because he loves me. He went on to say when you love someone you can show them your penis. His mum says so.

Overtures to other children need to be differentiated from the normal curiosity between children regarding differences between boys and girls. If children are involved in overtly bullying another child to participate, attempting penetration or putting objects inside each other's genitals or anus, this needs to be followed up.

Indicators which are not in the red alert section include situation-specific fears, such as bathtimes, toileting and bedtimes. These are often the contexts that are exploited by individuals who have a sexual interest in children. Children can also show person-specific fears. For example, Jasmine was afraid to be bathed only by her father. When anyone else bathed her, she was fine; when her father bathed her she was frightened. Over time this fear can become generalised. Norleen's fear of going to the toilet became so severe that she became frightened to go at all. It was often when she was going to the toilet that she would tell her mother that daddy had hurt her bottom. In both cases the situation-specific fears suggest that some inappropriate touching occurred in these contexts. They are green indicators because there are benign explanations – it could have been, for example that Jasmine's distress was a result of her disliking the way her daddy washed her hair, or that Norleen's distress was to do with the way her daddy wiped her bottom.

Developmental regressions, where a child returns to a previous stage of development (e.g. bed-wetting when they have been previously dry), is another sign of stress. It is considered a blue sign because children in this age range frequently show developmental regression to a wide range of stressors including, for instance, the birth of a sibling. Equally low on the index is aggressive, withdrawn or clingy behaviour. These are all indicators of stress, but in and of themselves are not indicative of sexual abuse.

Jasmine showed a whole range of symptomatic behaviours from across all three categories of risk. Before making a verbal disclosure, she demonstrated compulsive masturbatory behaviour, night terrors, fear of being bathed – especially by her father – fear of going to the toilet, aggressive behaviour, a degree of self-injurious behaviour – hitting and punching herself – bed-wetting, increased clinginess to her mother, and chronic urinary infections. Together all these indicators gave a picture of high risk which was later confirmed by her verbal disclosure and medical evidence.

If sexual abuse is suspected and reported to the statutory child protection agencies, the child is likely to be given a formal interview. Often the clear disclosures made to primary caregivers are not repeated to the formal investigators. This was the case for Evelyn, the little girl who disclosed to the nursery worker.

Even with such a clear disclosure, 'Daddy fuck my bum', investigators would need to know who daddy was (bearing in mind that some children have more than one daddy), what 'fuck' meant to this child and where she thought her bum was.

Children in this age range are likely to use idiosyncratic words to describe private parts. A primary caregiver is likely to know what the words are. Norleen and Heston's mother, for example, confirmed that 'ting-a-ling' was the word used in their family for penis. Young children may also use metaphors like 'snake' or 'stick' for penis, or not possess the proper word for genitals. However they are often very clear with gestures and pointing as to which part of their body, or someone else's body, they are referring to.

This in part is why dolls with genitals are sometimes used in interviews with children of this age. They act as an aid to discussion regarding touching.

> We had, like, dolls and everything and you had to show what they did. I didn't actually want to show them but, like, I thought it's a better way – like using dolls, than just speaking it – 'cause say there was a bit you wouldn't – you didn't want to say – you could, like, show it instead.

> (Natasha)

Some investigators are concerned that anatomical dolls are suggestive to children, causing them to verbalise or indicate something sexual has taken place when it has not.[1] But with training and an open mind they can be very helpful with young children. Additionally the spontaneous comments children make can add weight to the suspicions of sexual abuse. For example, this is taken from a four-year-old's interview:

> Following naming private parts and a general discussion regarding who can and cannot touch children's private parts the child begins to discuss the allegation of sexual abuse.

Q: Has anyone ever touched your mary?
Bonnie: Daddy has.
Q: Daddy has. Can you show me on the little dolly, how Daddy touched you?
Bonnie: He went like that. [Demonstrates with hand over vagina.]
Q: When Daddy touched your mary, was that a good touch or a bad touch?
Bonnie: A hurt touch.
Q: A hurt touch.
Bonnie: And it stinged.

Although the beginning of this sequence starts with a 'leading' question (i.e. a question that suggests something has happened), the prior context allowed for benign genital contact to have occurred between parent and child. The child had shown some confusion about who is and is not allowed to touch private parts. This is developmentally appropriate as children in this age range still may have adults helping them when it comes to toileting experiences. It is interesting, though, that the child names 'daddy' as the person who touches her private parts rather than mummy, who would for the most part be the parent involved in toileting. In response to the multiple choice question about good or bad touching the child provided her own choices: a hurting touch, and it 'stinged'. This is very significant because neither of these options was suggested by the interviewer, and they suggest some distress on the child's part regarding the touching. However it is still not conclusively indicative of sexual abuse because it is possible that the hurting and stinging could be a result of, for example, an episode of diarrhoea.

Q: Did you tell anyone when Daddy touched you and hurt you?
Bonnie: I told Aunt Cathy and Mummy. I won't let him do it again.
Q: Did Daddy tell you not to say anything?

Bonnie: Yup. He said 'You don't tell anyone or if you do you're not coming to my house any more. Or nanny's house.' [Bonnie's parents were separated.] Don't tell him.

Q: Don't tell him?

Bonnie: 'Cause he thinks no he didn't do it.

Q: He thinks he didn't do it.

Bonnie: But he did –

Q: But he did . . .

Bonnie: I didn't do anything naughty.

Q: And you didn't do anything naughty.

Bonnie: No . . . he's just fibbing.

Q: He's just fibbing, is he?

Bonnie: Don't tell him the bits I said. You just say 'Why did you do that to Bonnie?'

Q: I must ask him why he did that to you?

Bonnie: Write this down. [Child gives interviewer a pencil and starts to dictate a message to Daddy.] To say – you smack his face and then get out.

Q: Smack his face?

Bonnie: Yes, 'cause he's naughty. [The child then begins to play out giving Daddy her message. She draws a picture of Daddy's house.] And here's a bell. It goes ring. Ring ring.

Q: Who's going to answer the door?

Bonnie: Daddy or Joan [Daddy's new partner]. And you say 'Look at this message.'

Q: What is the message?

Bonnie: I'll say . . . you say . . . well, it's from Bonnie and she wants it for you and don't hang up.

Q: This is not for hanging up.

Bonnie: And then after . . . if he takes a seat you take a seat. When he says . . . when you want to go, you go . . . you say 'You're naughty 'cause you done that to Bonnie . . .' just stand there on the step [i.e. don't go in the house]. Just say to him 'This is for you and you don't come and see Bonnie.' And when you've finished with it come over to my house and give it to me.

This long and detailed transcript gives a flavour of the kind of information children in this age range give in formal interviews. There is not a lot of specific detail regarding the allegation itself. This partial transcript in and of itself is not sufficient to feel confident that a crime has been committed. But together with additional supporting information on her behaviour, the details of what she told Aunt Cathy and some of the qualitative material in her formal interview, the likelihood of sexual abuse by her father is high.

This interview also shows that the child's primary preoccupations are not with what has happened but what will happen in the future. Hence the urgency regarding the message to daddy. This is a very common preoccupation for children.

Here is another example from Heston and Norleen's interview. The little boy (Heston) is six years old and has Down's Syndrome. His sister (Norleen) is three. Heston has just hurt his finger in the door.

Q: Does it hurt?
Heston: How did I do it?
Q: You caught it in the door.
Heston: Silly.
Q: Was that silly?
Heston: Yes!
Q: Anywhere else hurts?
Heston: [Pointing at the doll's penis] That . . . ting-a-ling. It hurts. Look [touching the doll's penis] – *hurts*.
Q: Oh, dear. Who hurts your ting-a-ling?
Heston: Daddy.
Q: Your daddy does.
Heston: Yes! Him touch her bottom [pointing to his sister].
Q: Daddy touches Norleen's bottom.
Norleen: Yes [very quietly and turning away].
Q: Show me on the doll what he does.
Norleen: Daddy touch my bottom. [Child places hand over vagina of small doll; puts her finger in vagina of doll.]
Q: Did you like what he did?

Norleen: No. It hurt. Daddy hurt my bottom.

When these children saw their father for a supervised court-ordered access visit, they repeated their allegations to him. Heston immediately pointed to his father's genitals and started shouting 'Bite it, bite it.' Norleen was very defiant and directly confronted her father, saying 'You hurt my bottom. You are a naughty piggy.' During a game, both children had father lie down on the floor whilst they at first playfully hit him. Norleen said, 'I am going to make you bleed like Jesus.' (It was soon to be Easter.) She began hitting her father tentatively with a soft toy, changed to her shoe and then started to use her fists, slowly working from his feet until she delivered a vicious punch to his genitals.

Again, the amount of verbal material alone would not be considered sufficient to draw a conclusion. However, coupled with additional material, as well as the children's emotional response to the supervised access session, there is a strong likelihood of sexual abuse.

Children of this age provide a very limited amount of detail in formal interview settings. Primary caregivers usually give much greater information and often provide better quality material regarding the child's concerns and their behaviours.

Five to twelve age group

This is a large age span. However, children in this age range will know right from wrong, and will be able to understand about secrets and threats. Clearly there will be many of the same indicators as in the previous age group but the older age range leads to slightly different presentations.

Any verbal indication that sexual abuse is happening constitutes a red alert sign, and should be taken very seriously. It is very unlikely that children make up allegations of sexual abuse.

Children in this age range frequently tell other children rather than adults. In a study on prevalence of sexual abuse, Kelly, Regan and Burton found that 50 per cent of their sample who disclosed sexual abuse told either a relative or a close friend.[2] Often adults find out because the confidant tells a teacher or their parent. It is important that indirect or third-party disclosures are followed up by an adult, and that the child who has been sexually abused is spoken to. It would probably be helpful to have the confidant present when you talk to the child if this is practical. Repeated disclosures to a number of adults or over a period of time should be given weight.

Children in this age range clearly give more detail in their disclosures. They can also use grown-up words incorrectly. For example, one young girl told her mother she had had sexual intercourse with a friend's father when she was staying overnight. Medical examination revealed she had not been penetrated and was still a 'virgo intacta'. When questioned more closely by her mother, and asked to describe what had taken place, she stated clearly, 'He put his penis between my legs and moved it up and down.' She believed this to be sexual intercourse.

Children in this age range can also describe their experience metaphorically. They may say, for example, that they have been stabbed. Whilst it is important to check that this is not the case, it is equally important not to be too preoccupied with the literal description (i.e. if there is no knife, then the disclosure is wholly untrue).

These children can use many different ways of disclosing indirectly. They may tell obliquely by referring to a friend who has a problem, or by writing about it in creative projects at school. Such fictional accounts need to be taken seriously. The child or young person is almost certainly 'testing the water' regarding adult reactions to what is being said or hinted at. They are asking for information about what might happen as a result of disclosure. It is important for adults to know the possible procedures if sexual abuse is disclosed. If you work with children, you should also be sure that you are aware of policies and procedures at your workplace should a child disclose any kind of abuse to you.

Children frequently want adults they turn to for help to keep the sexual abuse secret. You will have to decide if this is something you can do. If you are in a professional role in relation to a child, you would almost certainly be advised to inform the statutory child protection workers. If you are a friend of the family or a parent, it is important for you to remember that secrecy rarely protects. You should share your concern with another trusted adult and together plan what you are going to do.

Many protectors think confronting the alleged perpetrator is the best way to intervene. This is unlikely to help unless you have already told others who support you in your confrontation. If the only person you tell is the alleged perpetrator, you can inadvertently increase the risk for the child because you will have alerted him to the child's attempt to get help. It is much better to tell someone who will believe what the child has said and support you in protecting the child from any further abuse.

Physical signs are harder to detect in this age range without a specific medical examination, because adults have much less benign contact with older children's private parts. Injuries and/or infections can easily be missed. If they *are* noticed, or a child complains about being sore, this should be followed up. There may be a benign explanation for it but it is important to consider sexual abuse as one possible explanation in the absence of a credible alternative.

For young girls at the top end of this age range, becoming pregnant as a consequence of sexual abuse is a possibility. Many adults do not consider pregnancy in this age range so it can go undetected until it has progressed considerably, often committing the girl to giving birth. It is important to recognise that any pregnancy in this age range is irrefutable proof that a criminal offence has taken place. And advanced technology makes it possible to prove beyond a shadow of doubt who the father of the child is or is not, provided both parties are prepared to give a blood sample.[3]

Sexualised behaviour and compulsive masturbation are

more common than pregnancy in this age range. At this age most children will have learned about what is considered appropriate behaviour, so inappropriately sexualised or masturbatory behaviour is a particularly strong sign of sexual abuse. Sexual overtures are unmistakable, with children making specific requests for sexual contact from adults or from other children. If the child has been sexually abused from a young age, she or he may still not really understand what is wrong with sexual activity, and may also have begun to see sexual contact as the way to negotiate life.

For older children who have not been abused from a young age, sexualised behaviour is less likely to occur until they reach the top end of this age range, where there is a developmental increase in sexual awareness anyway. Odd signals about sexual knowledge should be taken seriously at this age. It is difficult for children who have experienced sexual abuse to assess what they should or should not know and making a judgement about what constitutes common knowledge regarding sex and sexual contact is likely to be problematic for them.

Children who draw attention to their genitals by exposing themselves are also indicating to adults that this part of their body is overly important. All children know they have genitals; only a small minority think they should display them to others. Most will feel appropriately private about their bodies. Often the 'flashing' is done in contexts where adult supervision is absent or diffuse. For example, at playtime at school. Adults hear about it because other children complain, or because it becomes the focus of attention. Often it is dealt with by ignoring the behaviour itself and trying to distract other children. Whilst this may be appropriate at the time, it is important that it is followed up sensitively, both with the child and with the child's primary caregivers.

It can be difficult to assess what constitutes inappropriate sexual knowledge for this age range. At this age children naturally become more aware of aspects regarding reproduction, for instance. Issues regarding how the baby gets into and out of 'mummy's tummy' become more the focus, and this is of course not an indicator of sexual abuse. It can be helpful, therefore, to be conscious of how much sexual information is likely to have reached the children you are in contact with. Some will have come from family sources, so it is easy to have a sense of how much knowledge is passed on in this way. Children will also be talking about sex with their friends and possibly receiving some education from school on the facts of life.

Most parents do not give explicit sexual information to their children, and what they are likely to receive from friends or school is quite predictable. Clearly a child who describes a variety of sexual acts has developmentally inappropriate sexual knowledge. If this is coupled with experiential knowledge, such as, for example, texture, taste and smell, this is likely to be evidence of sexual experience which constitutes abuse. In the absence of the experiential knowledge, it is possible that a child may have received their information from pornographic films. But an accidental viewing is unlikely to result in a conversational knowledge of sexual activities; and if a child has been deliberately exposed to pornographic films then this constitutes non-contact sexual abuse.

Children in this age range who are being sexually abused may be experiencing feelings of helplessness and entrapment. If they dare not tell other adults what is happening then they have to learn to live with the abuse until they are old enough to escape from it themselves. (This process is described by Roland Summit as 'The Accommodation Syndrome'.[4]) As a consequence children can and do develop intense feelings of despair which can be difficult for them to articulate.

> I just – when he was doing it to me I just lost all communi-
> cation. I didn't talk to him – I just wanted him to leave me
> alone.
>
> (Alison)

I didn't really want to show it 'cause, like, I didn't want anyone to know – I was scared for anyone to know.

(Natasha)

Such children can't speak out, and protecting adults must be prepared to look for other signs such as behavioural disturbances.

Sometimes the child will attempt suicide, but this can be easy for the adult to miss, often because the attempts are unsuccessful and do not resemble adult attempts. Children in this age range will often try to kill themselves by doing expressly what they have been told not to do. For example, they may cross the road unsafely, or take things that are locked away because they are dangerous, like bleach. They may take tablets but often the tablets taken would not kill and consequently the adults around them do not recognise the overdose as a suicide attempt. They may try to drown or smother themselves. They may do very dangerous and reckless things. In the next age range, their attempts to kill themselves are usually more recognisable, but that can be because the suicide attempts began in *this* age range, and their technique has become more deadly as they have grown older.

Equally, children in this age range may begin to run away. When they are very young, adults can consider this to be simply wandering off. But home should be where children run to; if they do not, adults should begin to ask why.

Often it is within this age band that alcohol and drug use starts. Frequently it is the perpetrator who introduces the drink or drugs. They can do this to make it easier to overcome their targets, as well as increasing the young person's dependence on them. One ten-year-old girl, Tina, described her experience with hard drugs very clearly: 'First it was drugs and then "rudies", then it was "rudies" first before drugs.' She drew a picture depicting the 'before' and 'after' feelings from drugs, describing the drugged experience as producing a lift or 'floaty' feeling.

Children can find that such substances provide a means

of escaping, forgetting or self-medicating for their painful, disturbing and confusing experiences of sexual abuse.

> I started drinking when I was 11 with Martini, always out of the bottle, then I went on to Bacardi and vodka when I was 13 . . . alcohol was my only escape. It solved *everything*. I couldn't feel anything and nothing registered to my mind or my body. I drank in the morning, in the afternoon quite a lot, but mostly in the evenings at the pub or in the car.
>
> (Lisa)

So, drug and alcohol use can be indicators of abuse in this age range particularly, and protectors should always consider this as a possibility when discovering a child is using these substances.

Unexplained large sums of money and gifts should also make protectors wary, especially if they are given directly to the child without parental knowledge. These gifts can act as bribes and/or 'hush money' for keeping the inappropriate sexual contact secret. Many sexual offenders will also give gifts to the child's caregiver. They might offer to babysit or take the children away on holidays or other unsupervised activities that do not include the primary caregiver. Some offenders deliberately target those living below the poverty line, where such offers can be even more difficult to turn down and can seem very helpful at the time.

Children often understand the role that gifts to their parents play in the sexually abusive experiences. They recognise the often very real difference this makes to the family's overall standard of living, and the fact that such gifts make the sexual offender seem a paragon of virtue.

The behaviours described in detail above constitute the red alert signs for this age group. The most likely hypothesis for their existence is that sexual abuse is occurring, especially if there are a number of them present. The perpetrator is less likely to be a family member as children in this age range have greater mobility. But the younger the child, the more likely it is that the perpetrator will be from the child's immediate family network.

Other serious behavioural disturbances that may be correlated to experiences of sexual abuse are: hysterical symptoms (where the child seems to have a physical inability which has no medical cause, such as blindness or paralysis); anorexia and other eating disorders;[5] bed-wetting, especially if the young person has previously been dry; soiling and messing with poo; obsessional washing and cleaning; night terrors or sleep problems, especially if these have not been a continuous feature of the child's development; fire setting; and glue sniffing.

Clearly sexual abuse is not the only explanation for these behavioural disturbances. However it is important to remember that a child is communicating something by their behaviour. It can be useful to ask yourself, as a possible protector, what this child is trying to tell you by their behaviour that they cannot tell in words.

Q: Do you think there might have been any signs or clues that you were being sexually abused before you told?

Alison: My behaviour at school. The teacher just said that sometimes he felt like just taking me and shaking me. My mum just put it down to – 'cause she was pregnant with my sister – that she just thought it was jealousy. I just weren't doing nothing – sitting there, and if he told me to do my work I'd just look at him. My behaviour round the other children as well – I didn't want to play with them, didn't want to go near them. And what made it worse, my teacher was a man, and I just – I'd just, like, sit in the corner and isolate myself from the rest of the class. So he told my mum. He just called my mum up and my mum said they came to the decision that it was because of my little sister. They should have asked me.

I weren't as open as what I used to be – um, I was always sort of – hanging round her – if he come down – I was hanging round her – I didn't want to go out with him or nothing. Um – and when my sister was born I always used to try and make sure my mum was next to her, not him. I didn't want him going near her.

I used to scream at my little sister – towards my mum as well – she'd tell me to do something – I was standing there, like, you know – 'No, I'm not doing it. Do it yourself.' I started to blame her as well for not finding out what was going on.

Natasha: You can tell by, like, the way they act – 'cause like some of them might be petrified of men, so, like, they won't go near that man . . . you might have, like, acted different – you might have had nightmares, and dreams – some people wet the bed and everything.

Their education might, like, drop because they'll be scared of it and they might not want to eat, they might be sick, and 'I don't want to do this, I don't want to do that', they might stay in, they might stay in their bedroom, they might always want to be out – like, lots of things could be hints.

Q: Do you think you did any of these things?

Natasha: Yeah I did – dreams, wet the bed, everything.

Q: Did your mum notice these, do you think?

Natasha: If she noticed them I don't think she did anything, or like, whether it was like 'I can't be bothered.'

Some behaviours are very directly linked to the abuse. For example, if a child is regularly and repeatedly buggered by an abuser, then it is not surprising that the child soils and messes themselves. Similarly a child who is orally raped may develop an eating disorder.

Protectors need to recognise that there is a reason why a child behaves in the ways listed above. It is important to find out why these behaviours are happening, especially if commonsense approaches do not bring the behaviour under control. Asking about unwanted sexual experiences, especially if a child is clearly conveying distress through their behaviour, is extremely important. By guessing or discovering the clues, the adult relieves the child of both the burden of telling and the guilt for disobeying the injunction not to tell.

Twelve to sixteen age group

Sixteen is an arbitrary cut-off point but it is used because it coincides with the law regarding the age of consent for heterosexual activity. Under this age, sexual intercourse is not sanctioned by the law, and constitutes a sexual offence.[6]

Consequently pregnancy, terminations and venereal diseases in this age range all indicate a crime has been committed. They don't necessarily indicate abuse in the sense of non-consenting sexual intercourse, but there may well be a possibility that sexual abuse has happened when young women below sixteen become pregnant, or have a venereal disease.

Many young people who have been sexually abused become more sexually active than their peers. This can be a coping mechanism for surviving sexual abuse. For young women there is the fear that they will conceive a child from the perpetrator. By having sex with many men, the paternity of the child will be in doubt, and this may make the child easier to parent. This strategy – which may sound extreme to some – is in fact very frequently employed and described by young women.

Young people in this age range may decide they want to tell about the sexual abuse, and do so. Others blurt it out in a moment of weakness or anger. Or, they may make oblique reference to a past experience of sexual abuse in a vague or ambiguous way. For example, one young man hinted to his residential worker that he had previously been sexually abused. Correctly the worker followed up the hints.

In investigation the young man gave details with little prompting. He had clearly made a decision to tell.

Q: You know when you talked the other night to your keyworker about friends?

Keith: Yes.

Q: Could you tell us a bit more about it?
Keith: I don't want to get him in trouble and lose his job
– he's single and needs the money.
Q: Do you think you could tell us what happened?
Keith: Well, I woke up in the night, and I wanted a pill. I
forget what for now. I knocked on the sleeping-in room.
I remember it was one o'clock. Anyway I knocked on the
door and he opened it and asked what I needed. I asked
for a pill. He gave me a pill, then said, 'There is no point
in going back to bed now, you might as well come back to
bed with me.' I didn't really know what was going on . . .
he came to hug me from behind and . . . well . . . he did the
business.
Q: What do you mean by 'the business'?
Keith: Well, he bummed me.

This example shows some of the characteristics of disclosure
for a young person of this age. He had decided to tell. After
some hesitancy, he begins to tell of his experience. He remem-
bers details from the experience, such as the time in the morning, whilst at the same time he employs euphemisms to
describe his experience. Where a younger child might use
metaphor, an older child uses euphemism – in this case 'the
business'. Both are ways of distancing oneself from the reality
of the experience, especially the feelings that go with it.

Clearly, if a young person has not made a decision to tell,
and the experience of sexual abuse is disclosed accidentally,
the likelihood of retracting or taking it back is greater. However some young people experience pressure to retract from
their families, or feel so lonely and isolated when they are
away from their families that they are prepared to say it did
not happen when it did. If a young person retracts, protectors
should not consider the original allegations to now have no
substance.

There are situations where young women repeatedly make
'allegations' to the police, often about assaults by strangers,
which, when investigated, are found to be untrue. In many of

these cases the young woman has been previously sexually abused and has either not disclosed this, or has not been believed. Although the current details may not be true the disclosure of sexual abuse *is* essentially true. This is very serious and needs to be dealt with as it not only undermines the credibility of the young woman herself, but also of all women who report sexual crimes to the police. Often the young woman will eventually disclose her earlier experience of sexual abuse, but in such instances she is much less likely to be believed.

These issues are raised as indicators of sexual abuse because they are part of the more complex disclosing process in this age range. Retractions and false allegations of sexual crimes are both very unusual. They are most likely to occur in young people who have been sexually abused but who are not yet ready to be clear about their experiences or the identity of the perpetrator.

Young people of this age who have been sexually abused may be experiencing a range of distressing and disturbing behaviours. They can take some of their feelings out on others (externalising), or take them out on themselves (internalising). Often there is a gender difference, with boys usually externalising and girls internalising. Sexual offending behaviour against other children becomes much more apparent in this age range. If any child or young person is involved in sexually aggressive behaviour (including committing actual sexual offences), it is important that protectors consider that the juvenile perpetrator and sexual bully has been, or currently still is themselves, a victim of another perpetrator (usually an adult). This does not excuse their current behaviour but should alert protectors to look for an adult who has encouraged, and perhaps taught, the young person to behave in such ways. Many convicted adult male sexual offenders describe beginning their careers as sexual offenders at thirteen or fourteen years of age after themselves being victims of sexual offences.

Many sexually abused young women in this age group

become involved in prostitution. In the video 'A Crime of Violence', one young woman described prostitution as her way of gaining control over her experience.[7] She had been sexually abused and now she had sexual control of her male clients. But she also recognised that the men had the money to buy her if they chose to, and that therefore the sense of control was false.

As well as gaining a sense of control, abused young women may also have to turn to prostitution to earn money to support alcohol and drug addictions gained as a result of sexual abuse.

Young people who have been sexually abused over long periods of time do not view sexual contact as a way of expressing love and emotional intimacy. Instead, sexual contact can be seen as a means of expressing power and control.[8] High levels of sexual activity, with or without the exchange of money, are a strong indication that sexual abuse may have occurred.

It is possible for a young person who has been sexually abused to become addicted to the heightened arousal the abusive experience produces. They can then feel a physiological need to have sexual contact which is divorced from any emotional closeness. The young person is also likely to be confused about their physical feelings and may not label or recognise their sexual feelings as sexual, or may mistakenly label anxiety and fear as sexual feelings.

There are also gender differences in relation to what is considered appropriate sexual activity for this age range with boys given more freedom for sexual exploration with girls, than vice versa. Being treated and used as a sexual object by other people is extremely damaging. Many young people take their angry feelings out on themselves by mutilating and hurting themselves physically.

I used to, and sometimes still do, cut myself when I am frustrated, angry or upset because of what happened. When I am frustrated it lets the tension out to see the blood. When I feel guilty about what happened and scared that it will happen again I cut myself so I am uglier and so that it doesn't happen again. I cut myself when I am not sure how to cope with my anger. I can never direct my anger at the appropriate person so I cut myself ... Cutting is a sort of release – it's like taking all the bad out of your body, all the crap that's been left behind for *me* to deal with.

(Lisa)

This can happen in the younger age range but most frequently comes to adult attention in this age range. It is important to differentiate between self-inflicted cuts to kill and those meant to injure and hurt. They are conveying different messages. Cuts to harm are generally made on such parts of the body as the arms, legs, face, stomach or back. They are not directed at arterial points which, if cut, could result in bleeding to death.

Suicide attempts in this age range more closely resemble adult attempts (and it can often be in the context of recovering from a suicide attempt that a young person discloses for the first time).

Equally serious are breakdowns where a young person cuts him or herself off from the outside world, remaining mute or suffering from a serious psychiatric disorder. These consequences are often signs that the young person has suffered a severe trauma such as a violent rape, or protracted undiscovered sexual abuse.

Many of the serious problems discussed in the previous section are also relevant for this age group. Mental health practitioners and adult caregivers need to ask why a child or young person should manifest any serious disturbance. Neither children nor adults behave in this fashion for no reason. The older a child gets, the easier it can be to concentrate on what the child is doing rather than why the child is doing it. It is crucial to ask why at every age. Many factors could be responsible, such as death in the family or severe marital disharmony, but the possibility of sexual abuse should never be ignored. Additionally, some disturbed behaviours can mean the young person is continuing to experience additional abuses and traumas in addition to the original one.

Children who have already experienced sexual abuse are more vulnerable to other sexual offenders, especially if the original abuse remains undisclosed. Many of the behaviours they display can increase their vulnerability. If they are drunk, or drugged, they will not be able to protect themselves. If they are on the run or sleeping rough they can be raped or sexually exploited in exchange for a safe place to sleep for the night. These are all additional episodes of abuse which will make recovery more difficult. If you are involved with a young person who is engaged in high-risk behaviours, it is important not to blame them completely for what has happened, but to recognise what has driven them to such extremes. Many of the young people in this age range will have been abused over a number of years and as a consequence will have learned to live with sexual abuse as an inevitable reality in their lives, especially if they are sexually abused by more than one person.

It is also essential to ensure that, as time passes, an episode of known sexual abuse is not forgotten or seen as irrelevant to the difficulties the young person may have later in life. This often happens, especially with adult survivors who are presently in mental health facilities. Their current problems are often construed as being disconnected from experiences of childhood sexual abuse.

This age range has more green indicators because the number of possible explanations for distressing behaviours is much greater. Some of the green indicators may have appeared in the red alert section in a younger age range – pregnancy being an example. In trying to assess the weight of any one indicator, it is vital to consider a range of explanations, including sexual abuse. If another explanation seems to fit the current difficulties and there is some improvement following a tackling of the alternative reason, then that explanation may be correct. However, if a number of explanations have been used and lots of interventions have been tried, and yet challenging behaviours continue, it may be that adults have not considered sexual abuse.

It can be very frustrating if you suspect abuse, but the young person will neither confirm nor refute your suspicion. In these cases it can be helpful to discuss protection issues, to be clear that the young person's safety is important to you, and that you want to help them feel confident and secure in who they are and where they are going.

Following up Your Concerns

In using the list of indicators, it can be helpful to talk over your observations or concerns with another adult you trust. Many protectors correctly identify indicators but often play down or dismiss their significance. Then, with the hindsight a disclosure gives, the indicators are remembered clearly.

Alison's teacher and mother thought something was not right but they convinced themselves that it was to do with Alison's jealousy of her younger sister. Of course, once her mother knew what was wrong, a host of other odd incidents fell into place.

If you are seriously concerned about a child or young person you know, and they have not disclosed clearly to you, it can be helpful to record your observations in a diary. Try to describe accurately what you saw, use the child's words if they tell you something, note anything you thought odd or unusual. If you discuss your concerns with someone else, especially with a professional, make sure they record them and their advice to you (especially if they tell you not to worry and it later transpires you should have). A single episode of distressing behaviour (unless it involves a clear disclosure which is unambiguous, or a genital injury) is rarely a cause for concern. It is important that you trust your judgement and your knowledge of the child or young person. Noticing children's behaviour and acting on 'funny feelings' is part of protecting children.

SIGNS AND INDICATORS OF CHILD SEXUAL ABUSE

Under 5's	5-12 Years	12+
RED	**RED**	**RED**
Disclosure	Disclosure	Disclosure
Genital injuries	Genital Injuries	Genital Injuries
VD	VD	Self-mutilation of breast/genitals
Vivid details of sexual activity (such as penetration, oral sex, ejaculation)	Sexual stories/poems	Pregnancy/under 14
Compulsive masturbation (contextually abnormal)	Sexual drawings	VD – under 14
Sexual drawings	Exposing themselves	Prostitution
sexualised play usually acting out explicit sexual acts	Masturbation in contextually inappropriate fashion	
	'Promiscuity'	
	Suicide attempts	
	Running away	
	Alcohol and drug abuse	
		GREEN
GREEN	**GREEN**	Sexual boasting/stories/jokes
Person specific fear	Arson	VD – over 14
Nightmares	Soreness of genitals/bottom	Pregnancy – over 14
Chronic urinary/vaginal infections	Chronic urinary/vaginal infections	Sexual offending
Soreness of genitals/bottom	Obsessional washing	Rebellious against men (specific gender)
Situationally specific fears –	Depression	Drug and alcohol abuse
Fear of being bathed	Hysterical symptoms	Suicide attempts
Fear of being changed	Enuresis	Self mutilation
Fear of being put to bed	Encopresis	Continual lying
	Anorexia	Truanting
	Glue sniffing	Running away
	Nightmares	Hysterical symptoms
	Truanting	Obsessional washing
	Unexplained large sums of money/gifts	Psychotic episodes
BLUE		
Developmental regression	**BLUE**	**BLUE**
Hostile/aggressive behaviour	Abdominal pains	Depression
Psychosomatic condition	Developmental regression	Anorexia
	Peer problems	School refusing
	Psychosomatic conditions	Peer problems
	School problems	Authority problems
		Delinquency
		Psychosomatic conditions

*KEY: RED — High Probability
          GREEN – – Moderate Probability
          BLUE – – – Low Probability

CHAPTER THREE

Reducing the Risks and Helping Children to Tell

This chapter will deal with ways to reduce the risk of sexual abuse. It contains useful information to give children in advance in case sexual abuse happens; encourages you to consider ways of talking about concerns you might have about a child or young person; and discusses how you should deal with a child telling you about sexual abuse.

The adults most closely connected to children, their primary caregivers, have a greater impact on children's recovery than professionals alone. Only in a minority of cases do children need to talk about sexual abuse with professional helpers. A believing and supportive adult, especially a primary caregiver, makes all the difference for a good recovery from the experience of sexual abuse. Consequently learning how to talk about 'it', in case and preferably *before* 'it' happens, following up your concerns and feeling confident about what you might do if a child discloses to you are necessary skills for all protecting adults. Good communication skills are essential. This involves not only being able to talk about sexual abuse but also listening carefully, observing and commenting about what you see and hear.

It will be helpful to talk about sexual abuse with other adults first so that you can identify a receptive network of support for yourself in case you have to help a child or someone you love recover from the experience. If helpers don't have anyone to talk to, they can begin to feel overburdened by the awfulness and sometimes feel unable to listen to any more details about sexual abuse. This can apply just as much to professional helpers as to caregivers. Also, if you cannot think of anyone you could talk to about something like this, it will be hard for you to convey the need for openness to your children. Children will recognise your difficulty and continue to try to protect you from their experience.

Many adults wonder when to begin giving their children information. Whilst it may seem best to wait until children ask, this can be a risky strategy. Children will assume that all adults are going to be safe and that what they do is always right. They are dependent on their primary caregivers to help them shape their understanding of the world. So the earlier you start to talk to them, the better. The following outlines some issues you can discuss, even with very young children.

'Keeping safe'

When your child goes to school, 'keeping safe' may be part of the school curriculum. It can help for you to know how the school will introduce the topic to your child, so that you can reinforce the messages at home. If the school does not offer this as part of the curriculum, you should encourage them to do so. There are a number of safety programmes designed for use in schools.[1]

Body awareness

For the very young, or those who will not be able to articulate their experiences, it will be important to listen and observe their behaviour. These children are more likely to tell you things through showing you. Giving children a language to talk about their bodies is the first step. Most families have words for private parts and become involved in discussing toileting with little ones before this becomes a private activity. Developing a language to talk about bodies is a good first step towards the more complex discussion about unwanted touching.

It is important to watch how other adults and children interact with your child. Sometimes adults can be overinsistent on cuddles and kisses. If a child says no to unwanted hugs and kisses it is important not to try and insist that they accept them. If you do, you will be conveying the message that the child cannot make their own judgements about what is pleasurable and what is not, and that they don't have the right to say no.

If your child has a physical disability which means that

regular physical contact by another is necessary, it is important for the child to be able to indicate what they like or dislike about other people's handling of them. Clearly verbal skills help, but children can also convey satisfaction or dissatisfaction with the way in which they are being handled non-verbally, by crying out or pulling away when they don't like it.

Knowing your child's social network and surroundings

Part of protecting children is knowing where they are, who they are with, where they are going and what they are doing. Young children often have a very limited circle of friends, adult carers and places to go but as a child moves away from the home into nursery school, playgroups, or to be with babysitters or childminders, it is important that you have enough information about the adult caregivers to whom you are entrusting your child's care. If your child is being looked after by someone else, how well do you know that person? Have you been clear to childminders about what you consider acceptable behaviour in relation to discipline? And about whether the child can be taken out and if so, under what conditions? What other adults and children may they come into contact with? By discussing these matters with caregivers you can convey that you take the protection of your child seriously and that you want other adults to do so as well.

It is important that you check with your child how their time away has been, not in an inquisitorial style but out of interest, and to reassure yourself they have been safe and secure. Making such discussions a usual part of life also lays down the foundation for the future, when much more autonomous behaviour is developmentally appropriate, such as children going to school on their own, going out with friends, or on school trips.

You should also use the individual names of adult caregivers, rather than a general title like teacher. This ensures you and your child can be clear about who is being discussed.

Types of touching

It is important to talk to children and young people about appropriate and inappropriate touching. Such discussions can start at a young age and be adjusted as the child gets older. Then if an incident of unwanted touching does occur, you will be more confident about how to talk about it. If you are used to the subject you will also be able to convey the necessary under-reaction that allows children to carry on speaking about what has happened.

You may want to start with something simple like bad and good touching, which includes hitting, kicking, punching, biting and scratching, as well as kisses, cuddles, snuggles, hugs. As the child gets older you should incorporate ideas about their body being their own, and encourage the child to develop a sense of privacy or body space. Children with severe physical disabilities will need to have this message modified.

Children may enjoy playing with their genitals, often taking no notice of when or where. It is important that the child receives a message from parents and other caregivers about when and where they should enjoy the pleasures of their own bodies. If they continue to do so publicly they may be at risk, as this provides a perfect opening for someone interested in sexual offending against children.

Similarly young children can express an interest in touching or looking at adults' genitals, often in the context of going to the toilet or bathing.[2] This can begin to feel uncomfortable and most caregivers will assert their right to privacy. Children can benefit from hearing their parents model assertive behaviour in relation to touching. This helps children learn both to give and to receive comments about touching.

If you are clear about what you consider appropriate touching, and your child has experience of you giving feedback to other adults and children, they will be more likely to use you as a source of help if they have a problem with unwanted or confused touching. Concentrating on touching is better than trying to identify potential abusers, as this focus offers the greatest protection, does not exempt anyone, and encourages children to judge each situation for themselves.

Secrets

Because so many sexual offenders tell children to keep the abuse secret, you may want to think about how you would counteract this message or enable your child to be confident enough *not* to keep the secret.

Very young children, under the age of three, do not really understand what a secret is. For older children, you may want to encourage them to share their secrets with someone they trust. In this way, there can at least be an opportunity for someone else to know and to help decide if it is a secret that should be kept.

This may be very important as children grow up, as many children who have been sexually abused choose to tell other children first. This may mean that your child could be chosen as the confidant of another child. If they are at all unsure about keeping something secret, they should discuss it with another trusted person, preferably an adult. It can help to be clear that anything harmful should not be kept secret.

Encouraging children to tell

Clearly this is linked to all the other issues raised so far. It is important that children know that you want them to tell you if another child or an adult is hurting or upsetting them in any way. There may be some situations which are confusing rather than clearly hurtful. These need to be discussed as well.

In the first instance, you want to give your child the message that it is all right to talk to grown-ups about issues that concern the child or young person. You may also want to help them decide who in their current network is someone they could trust and talk to other than yourself. The identification of a range of protecting adults for children to turn to is extremely important. Sometimes children mistakenly think their parents would not be able to deal with their difficulties. And sometimes they are right.

Rehearsal

You may want to encourage your child to think what they might do if they were in certain hypothetical risk situations. This need not focus exclusively on sexual abuse. Parents or other primary caregivers could ask children what they would do if there was a fire alarm or if someone became very ill or hurt themselves very badly. This would make children more confident about dealing with risk situations in general so that they could know who to turn to and what to do if sexual abuse became an issue for them.

Helping children develop strategies for dealing with bullying, and sexual and racial harassment is also very valuable, even for children who may not themselves be the target. With these strategies a child observing an episode of bullying, for example, may feel more able to tell about it; and children will also be encouraged to protect one another. Also, successfully identifying bullying or harassing types of behaviours will be useful in helping children to recognise situations where hatred is allowed to flourish.

Helping children and young people assess when it is safe enough to challenge and confront is extremely important. It can be useful to explain that it is not the child's responsibility to change other people's prejudiced views, and that sometimes it is best to leave the situation rather than stay and try to sort it out.

Using books and other resources

Having books and other appropriate material conveys an openness regarding both sexual knowledge in general, and sexual abuse in particular. Some children prefer to read about it rather than to talk directly to an adult. It can be useful to check what material is available at your local libraries. If there is nothing for children, young people or adults on protecting children from sexual abuse, you may like to make some suggestions, and then to check regularly that the material is still available.

... My old school, they had on a wall somewhere **Child-Line** and the phone number ... the books about sexual abuse were only in the adult section ... and like, you really had to look to find them. I once stumbled across this book [on sexual abuse], and, like, half the pages were all missing. Someone had been ripping out pages and I was, like, trying to read it, and I was, like, 'Help' [so] I took it to the librarian ... and he goes, 'Oh, don't worry, most of the books are like that' – like he's not really worried.

(Natasha)

Try to read or see the material first before giving it to your children. Some material is very explicit or may give messages you do not agree with. If this is the case, you may find you cannot deal with the questions children may ask, or that the material is promoting a view you do not share. Much that is written or produced is not for all children. The material can be aimed at a particular age range or, more commonly, can assume that all children are white, and able-bodied.

Trying to address the issue of risk from close family members can be difficult. Using resources developed to help children and their caregivers talk about sexual abuse can make it easier as some of these books specifically mention family members.

You should use the intimate knowledge you have about your child to decide if short stories, colouring books, videos or a combination of all of these materials would be the most effective way to help talk about protecting your child from sexual abuse. A detailed list of resources is provided in the Appendix.

Following up Concerns

It is important that you follow up any concerns you have about children you care for or come into contact with. This can include concerns arising from your own observations or discussions with the child, even if it is not your own child. It can sometimes be easier for someone else to raise worries the primary caregiver may have noticed, but is not yet able to deal with.

You may notice children behaving sexually with one another. You will need to get the children to stop before you talk about it with them.

It may be obvious what the children were doing. It may seem harmless. On the whole adults do not worry about incidents where children seem to be exploring physical differences. However if the children have taken off their clothes, are putting things into each other's genitals or bottoms, or one child is clearly bullying another child into continuing, it is necessary for you to explain what is wrong about this kind of behaviour.

If the episode involves children from more than one family, it is important that you share your concerns with the other primary caregivers. This should include not only what happened but also how you managed it, including what you said.

When children are involved in incidents with other children, it can be difficult to decide if their contact is sexually abusive, especially if the age difference is very small. These are some of the things that can help you to decide.

- Is there a significant age gap (five years or more), or a marked imbalance between the children in physical size or intellectual development?
- Were any threats used in the incident? Any actual physical coercion?
- Was either of the children old enough to understand about right and wrong? Had either of the children been specifically told not to do this before?
- Was the episode conducted in a secret, covert way? Was there any evidence of premeditation – that one child had decided in advance what they were going to do?
- Have there been past episodes with either of the participants which might suggest a compulsive element to the behaviour?

If the answer is yes to a number of these questions, it is important that the caregivers follow up the incident with all the children involved, perhaps separately, and with their primary caregivers if it involves more than one family. This is especially important if there is a significant age gap, threats or overt coercion were used, and there was an element of premeditation. In these situations, it is likely that one of the children may have been taught to behave this way by an adult.

If you feel uncomfortable about some touching you observe between adults and children, it is important that you follow this up and do not pretend it did not happen, or that you misinterpreted it.

In Evelyn's case, her mother spoke to the nursery workers about her concerns regarding Evelyn's father. He used to take Evelyn into the bathroom and not let his wife, Evelyn's mother, in. Evelyn's mother pointed out to staff that Evelyn had a red, sore bottom on occasion. Evelyn's mother was clearly worried about her daughter but did not know how to voice her fears more directly. Perhaps she did not consider sexual abuse as a possibility. She needed someone to take her worries seriously and begin to ask questions regarding the behaviours that made her worry.

In Jasmine's case, both her mother and her maternal aunt noticed that Jasmine's father was excessive in his creaming of her genitals when she was a baby. However they did not talk about this with each other until Jasmine's behaviour became more distressed when she was older (about two and a half years), and she began to disclose. Both of them had discounted their observations and not challenged Jasmine's father about his behaviour at the time.

Vanessa's mother was extremely anxious that Vanessa was being sexually abused by Vanessa's father. She expressly asked Vanessa's father not to change the baby's nappy when he was left for short periods of time in sole charge. Despite her requests, he continued to change the child's nappy.

There were other indicators in all of these cases that were highly suggestive of sexual abuse. But in each case, while the primary caregivers were concerned about how the child was being handled, they were unable to follow up their concerns effectively.

This effective following up of concerns is especially important if you are in contact with a known sex offender – known either because he has a previous conviction or because you know personally that he has offended before. In these cases, it is important that you give your children explicit messages regarding this person and do not leave your children with him unsupervised. Many adult survivors of sexual abuse incorrectly assume that there is no risk to their children from their childhood perpetrator. But sexual offenders do not 'grow out of' sexual offending behaviour.

Knowing who to discuss these concerns with and having them taken seriously is a first step in effective protection and reduction of possible risk. You may want to discuss your concerns with other adults in your network, or with professionals who also know your child, such as your GP, health visitor, your child's minder, nursery worker or teacher. It is crucial that this person listens carefully to what you have to say and helps you to think of ways of monitoring the situation until the issues become clearer.

There are times when you may not be taken seriously. For example, when Vanessa's mother spoke to her GP about her concerns, he referred her for psychotherapy because of her obsession with the possibility that her daughter was being sexually abused! He did not consider that these concerns might be founded, did not implement any child protection procedures, nor suggested that a formal investigation might be appropriate.

However, when Jasmine's mother expressed her concerns to her GP, the doctor organised further follow-up including a medical examination. The findings of this examination confirmed Jasmine's mother's worst fears, but she was offered ongoing support for herself throughout and after the subsequent formal child protection investigation.

If as a primary caregiver you are dissatisfied with the response you receive when talking to professionals about your concerns, you should not hesitate to get a second opinion. You can use some of the phone lines or voluntary agencies to help you find someone who will take your concerns seriously. It may also be a good idea to take someone else with you when reporting your concerns. It can be helpful to have a clear description about any incident that is worrying, to be able to give details about what made this incident such a cause for concern, and outline what you did. It is important that your concerns are recorded, either by yourself or by the professional you have contacted.

If the child's behaviour becomes less worrying over time, it is likely that whatever was distressing the child has now stopped. However, if sexual abuse was happening, it is likely the child will continue to show signs of distress and cause you concern. If distressing behaviour continues you may want to obtain more specialist advice from child mental health workers. Your GP can refer you on.

If you find a plausible explanation for the child's behaviour, and you then try to rectify the situation, there should be some improvement in the child's behaviour if your explanation is correct. If there is no improvement, you may need to be more direct and ask the child what is bothering them.

> Don't make the mistake that my mum and teacher did. They should have asked me. Nobody said to me – they just come down to the decision that it was 'cause of my sister . . . Know your child . . . when something does go wrong, you will know what you're looking for . . .
>
> (Alison)

If the child can't or won't answer a general question, you may want to ask them about several specific possibilities, including unwanted touching. In all cases, trust your instincts and your knowledge of the child.

What to Do If a Child Chooses You to Tell

Before the situation arises, it is crucial that primary caregivers think about the possibility that a child may tell them about an incident of sexual abuse. The essential elements to convey to the child when an unambiguous disclosure of sexual abuse has been made are very straightforward. You want the child to know (a) that they were right to tell; (b) that you believe them; (c) that you are going to help them get it sorted out; (d) that the abuser was wrong to do that; (e) that it was not their fault; and (f) that you are sorry it has happened to them.[3]

If a child begins by asking you to keep something secret, it is important *not* to promise to do so. You need to know what they are going to say first before you can decide what you need to do. You may say you wouldn't want to make a promise you might not be able to keep. If the child does not say anything more because you won't keep it secret, you should encourage them to tell someone else and perhaps suggest a phone line such as ChildLine, where they can talk confidentially. You also need to be clear that you would really like them to feel able to talk with you and to trust your judgement about what would need to happen next if you felt you could not keep their secret.

Your immediate reaction to what the child says is important.

When I told her, she sort of like looked at me, you know – nothing . . . she just – just didn't want to know any more – like she just sat there, and I didn't know what to do – I'm just sitting on the opposite side and we started crying, and then she phoned the police . . . but she didn't talk to me. I was just sitting there on my own 'til they come . . .

(Alison)

If the child tells you that someone you are close to is the perpetrator, it can be very shocking, even unbelievable. Remember the courage it has taken for the child to tell you. If you let your feelings show too much this can be very inhibiting for the child or young person. They need you to be strong for them, to offer them comfort and support.

Sometimes this is not immediately possible because your grief or anger or shock is too much. In these cases, you will need to talk to the child later when you feel more in control. It will be important for you to be clear that you are not angry with the child. Having your own source of support is essential, so you should find an adult you trust to talk to as soon as possible, so that you can support your child in the way that is most helpful to them.

It may be tempting to get a verbatim record of what the child is saying by audio- or video-taping the discussion. This should be avoided for a number of reasons. Most importantly it would clearly interfere with the spontaneity of the child's telling. Caregivers do not generally record what children say to them. Organising a specific session so the child can say it all on tape will go against the child in a formal investigation, precisely because the primary caregiver will have had to set up the situation to record. It would also be unethical to record without the child knowing. It is much better to listen to the child, and ask a minimum of questions – just enough to be sure of what the child is saying and to help decide what needs to be done.

Do not probe unnecessarily or feel that the child needs to tell everything. It takes time for children to tell. They often begin with the least awful aspect and wait to see what the response is before revealing more details. So there is usually more to come.

However, if a child does start to tell a large number of details, it is not appropriate to stop them. You could take notes, telling the child that what they are saying is important. In this way you can reassure the child they are being taken seriously. The child's own words should be used – they should not be translated into adult language. If the child uses an idiosyncratic description, it can be helpful to ask them what they mean. Any non-verbal behaviour that goes with the telling should be noted, but no attempt should be made to interpret it. It is necessary only to get as much information as will be needed to know what to do next. Then the child should be told what will happen next.

If the disclosure is made to someone who has formal procedures to follow, such as a teacher, these should be outlined to the child or young person as well as to the primary caregiver. There is no mandatory reporting of child protection concerns in the United Kingdom but professionals involved with children or with adults where a child protection issue becomes apparent are strongly encouraged by the Department of Health to report their concerns to child protection agencies for further investigation. Only in exceptional circumstances, where the child's safety is at risk, should a formal investigation begin without the involvement, and consent of the primary caregiver.

Ideally a non-abusing parent will co-operate and help with a formal investigation. This includes giving permission for any necessary medical examination and investigative interview. Children need to know that it is all right for them to talk to professionals involved in the investigation and the child's caregiver should be sure to tell them this.

The investigation process is described in more detail in the chapter on using the statutory agencies (Chapter Seven).

Protecting the Child Immediately After a Disclosure

Your child's safety should come first. If someone within the family has been named as the perpetrator, the issue of removal may be raised by the professionals involved. Ideally the alleged perpetrator should move elsewhere. This does not suggest guilt but indicates that adults who care for the child recognise that it is less stressful for the adult to move out for the time being than it is for the child. If this is not possible, it is worth thinking of a member of the extended family that the child could stay with while the investigation is being conducted, or until the child's long-term protection is secured.

The child should not be badgered about what they have

said already, or be put under any pressure to discuss it in more detail. Additionally, they should only have supervised contact with the alleged perpetrator, if any at all. This is because many children are put under enormous pressure to retract or take back what they have said following a disclosure of sexual abuse which names someone. Sexual offenders use very subtle (and sometimes not so subtle) tactics to intimidate both adults and children alike.

Consequently telephone calls which are difficult to monitor should not occur; letters should be screened, with the awareness that they can be used to play on the child's loyalty and may contain coded messages; gifts are totally inappropriate and should not be allowed; actual contact should be supervised by someone who believes that the child may have been sexually abused, and who could intervene if they felt the contact was not appropriate. Inappropriate contact involves secrets being whispered, taking the child out of the room unsupervised (even to the toilet), and some forms of physical contact, such as sitting on the lap. If your partner is the subject of an allegation of sexual abuse he will need to think carefully about how to interact physically with your child in a way that conveys affection for them but does not bring you added concern.

When Vanessa's mother asked her partner not to change Vanessa's nappies, he should have followed her request as this would have shown his respect for her and that he could put Vanessa's protection first. This pattern of stubbornly continuing to do something that the child's mother has expressly asked not to be done is often a characteristic of sexual offenders. It is not a lack of control they are exercising but the opposite – a wilful defiance of parental authority and an attempt to continue to exert control over the child and over you.

If the named perpetrator lives in your family and does move out while the situation is being investigated, your other children will need to be told in an age-appropriate fashion why he is staying somewhere else for a while (see Chapter 4). They may be very shocked and react strongly by blaming their sibling for causing this disturbance. Almost always they will take their lead from the parent left in charge. It is important to remember that other children in the family may also have been sexually abused but decided not to tell. This can explain some of the very strong reactions siblings sometimes have. You should not make assumptions that only boys, or girls, or teenagers, or stepchildren will be targets in any one family. Once someone has violated one child, it is possible that they may violate others until they get the help they need to stop behaving in this way.

If the child protection services are involved they may ask for other children in the family to be interviewed or medically examined. This will be to assess the protection issues for all children in the family as well as offering other siblings a private forum where they, too, may disclose. Additionally, other children in the family may have information which supports or refutes what has already been alleged.

It is helpful if you can prepare the children for any medicals or interviews that may take place, and indicate clearly that it is all right to speak about family matters to the investigators. Without this permission it is very confusing, and unlikely that children will be able to say anything.

It is important to recognise that if a child is formally interviewed and then returned home to face their alleged perpetrator and continue to live with them while the investigation is going on, it is most unlikely they will repeat the disclosure which prompted the investigation, even if there is other evidence of sexual abuse, such as medical findings. They are very likely, in these circumstances, to retract or take back what they said.

Below is a list of reasons, generated in a girls' group, about why children do not tell:

1. Feel they won't believed.
2. Too scared.
3. Think it's their fault.
4. Think they'll get beaten up.

5. No one to tell.
6. No one to trust.
7. Don't know what will happen if they tell.
8. Scared Mum and Dad will turn against them.
9. Don't want the police involved.
10. Brothers and sisters might be put into care as well as them.
11. Think they are dirty.
12. Worried about what friends will say.
13. Don't want a medical examination.
14. Too young to know what's going on.
15. Wouldn't make a difference if they did tell.
16. Already tried to tell and nothing happened, so gave up.[4]

Children who have been sexually abused will almost certainly have been instructed not to tell. Often it is their mothers in particular who are singled out for exclusion by the perpetrator. Threats will have been made about what will happen if they do tell. This can include not being believed, being put in care, hurting their mother, and in some circumstances explicit threats of physical violence to the child and/or to people – or even pets – that they love.

Why I didn't want to tell:

1. George said he would kill me and I would be put in care.
2. I was scared mostly for my brother and sister.
3. I felt too dirty and ashamed to tell my mum.
4. I wouldn't have known how to tell her anyway because how do you tell your mum that her stupid boyfriend is messing around with her child's body when if anything it should be hers he's touching not mine.
5. At the time I was scared of being put in care so I thought it would be easier to run away.

(Karen)

It is necessary to remember that the threatening side of the person accused of sexual abuse will not necessarily be apparent to outsiders. Often, as long as they are in charge of things, their behaviour is charming. However, when discovered and confronted or challenged by others, they can become very bullying and abusive. In these circumstances, and together with the fear, confusion and distress that may follow a disclosure of abuse for all concerned, it is hardly surprising that children often don't want to repeat allegations, and sometimes try to withdraw them.

If a child chose you to disclose to, they did so for a reason. This may be because they think you will take them seriously, believe what they have to say, and help them try to sort out the situation. If you are not the child's parent you will need to make a decision about the best way to let the child's parents know what the child has said to you, and what you feel you should do with that information.

If you have any reason to believe that telling the child's parents might put the child at risk you should contact a child protection agency first, or an outside support service such as the church, a community group or adult friends who may be able to offer a safe place for the child while the issues are sorted out or looked into in greater detail.

It can be tempting to immediately confront the alleged perpetrator regarding the child's allegations. But remember, only a tiny minority of perpetrators admit that the child is telling the truth. Some sexual offenders will admit initially, promise never to do it again, and give many seemingly plausible reasons for why it happened in the first place; and then when they are no longer under scrutiny carry on with the sexual abuse.

This is not a problem that will go away. If you try to keep the issue of sexual abuse within the family and not involve outside sources of support for yourself, you are likely to be swayed by the entreaties of the other adult over time, and may end up convincing yourself that it did not happen, or that it has now stopped. Try to get some thinking space for both the child and yourself. The alleged perpetrator should be asked to spend some time separate from the rest of the family while decisions regarding the next step are made. The most important thing is to demonstrate that you and other protecting adults, who could be friends or relatives, are now in charge of the family.

If a child tells you about their experience of sexual abuse, they believe you will help them. They are also signalling to you that they want the sexual abuse to stop, and they need your help to stop it. Telling will be the first step for the child in moving from victim to survivor; believing and continuing to protect the child is your first step towards providing the best possible start for their recovery process.

CHAPTER FOUR

Establishing a Context for Recovery

It is helpful to recognise that if you are a non-abusing parent you are likely to be in shock if you hear of your child's disclosure or of a child protection agency's concern about your child. Help and support will be needed for you to come to terms with the possibility of sexual abuse of your child by someone you know, trust, and possibly love.

> Please someone listen to me, tell me why it happened? Why did I not see it happen? Why am I the only person going through this hell? That's what I used to think when I lost my children to child sexual abuse.[1]

Discovering that your child may have been sexually abused by a member of your family is like being confronted with an unexpected bereavement. The unexpected nature of the information makes it harder to deal with. Even if you had an inkling something was wrong, it is very shocking to discover that sexual abuse is at the bottom of that confusion.

When someone dies, there are social and cultural rituals which help the mourning process. However, because of the stigma attached to sexual abuse, families touched by it find it difficult to share with others. There are no rituals to help lessen the distress, and the sense of shame and isolation is often overwhelming, even to those parents who believe and protect their child immediately.

When confronted by an allegation which names someone you have known, possibly loved and trusted with your children, it takes a lot of courage to believe.

> It doesn't feel real. Every day is exactly like the next and on the outside nothing looks different. It wasn't until he

admitted it – until then it was just a horrible nightmare. I kept thinking 'There's no way it could be him. Somewhere there's got to be a guy in a dirty raincoat; because I've known this man all my life.'[2]

This chapter helps you establish and maintain a context for recovery from an experience of sexual abuse. Recovery is not just something your child needs to experience. Everyone in the family will be affected by the disclosure of sexual abuse and will need help coming to terms with it. The chapter looks at what your child needs from you, what you need for yourself, and what can get in the way of being an effective protector.

What the child needs

Your belief

Your child needs you to believe and support them. Despite your shock and confusion, you must put their need for safety and reassurance first. A protecting parent should be able to demonstrate unequivocally that they can protect their child and reduce the risk of any further sexual abuse.

We saw in the last chapter that if the alleged perpetrator is living within the family it can be extremely difficult to guarantee such protection and reduced risk. If the perpetrator remains living in the same family, continues to deny that sexual abuse took place, and consequently does not receive any help for his problem, then the risk of future abuse is extremely high, even with a believing non-abusing parent. In part, this is because the perpetrator will have undermined your child's confidence that you will be able to protect them.

If the child protection services are involved and no protectors can be identified within the child's immediate family, removal from the family home may be considered. The consequences of this, for the child, who may then believe that *they* are being punished, can be devastating. So it is important that you think how you will protect your child now and in the future.

In a situation with a named abuser, you need to:

1. Create a distance between the child and that abuser.
2. Surround the child with a supportive network of *believing* adults.
3. Give yourself time and space to let the fact of the abuse sink in.
4. Arrange support for yourself.

Mothers, as non-abusing parents, often carry the burden of guilt in sexual abuse. They are often also confronted with the starkest choices – their child or their partner.

Society confirms women who have relationships with men and actively encourages families to include both a male and a female parent. It is not surprising, then, that when women are confronted with that stark choice, they often opt for their partner. The economic dependence of mothers on fathers can be a very significant factor in deciding to disbelieve a child's allegations against their father. If you have never lived alone or been a single parent, it can seem an overwhelming prospect to contemplate.

Consequently it may seem easier to live with a 'child who lies' than to confront the issue of a partner who sexually offends against your children; or to accept the minimisations and rationalisations from the offender and believe that it won't happen again; or to hope that now it is out in the open it will stop.

If you are in the situation of hearing that your child may have been abused, and really can't believe it, use the list of indicators described in Chapter 2 to help you think about your child and the probability of sexual abuse.

If it comes to light and you can't believe it, just sit down and try to analyse things you may have been unsure about but didn't bother to question . . .

(Kiera)

If your child has a number of indicators then you should start asking questions, not of the possible perpetrator but of your child.

Sometimes hearing your child's account will help convince you that the sexual abuse must have happened. The child's use of language and the description of familiar places or events will all contribute to your belief in what they have said.

This may be especially important if your child has told someone else but not yet been able to tell you directly. If this is the case, you need to let your child know that you have been told what they have said, that you are glad they have told, and that you believe them. Disbelief by a primary caregiver is devastating for the child and seriously impedes the child's recovery.

Your understanding

To begin the recovery process, it is important that you are emotionally sensitive towards your child. This can be difficult because you will not only be in shock but may also be mourning the loss of a partner or experiencing a separation with an uncertain future.

Emotional sensitivity can also be difficult to achieve if your child's reaction to the sexual abuse does not conform to expectations. Many people expect children to show distress and rejection of the perpetrator. However it is important to recognise that some sexual offenders lavish attention, physical affection and possibly gifts on the child. They may also have given the child some positive parenting experiences in addition to sexually abusing the child. This makes it confusing both for the child and for the non-abusing parent.

If more than one child in your family has been sexually abused, they can react in totally different ways. One may be very quiet and withdrawn whilst the other may be very angry and acting out. A protecting adult must be prepared for a wide range of often conflicting emotions that may fluctuate over time.

If you have also experienced sexual abuse in your childhood, you may find it difficult to disentangle your feelings from those of your child. This new episode of sexual abuse may rekindle feelings you thought you had dealt with.

It can be especially devastating if your childhood perpetrator is also the perpetrator of your child's sexual abuse. You can feel you are to blame for your child's sexual abuse because you didn't tell when you were being abused. It is important to remember that you are not responsible for the perpetrator's actions.

If you find yourself overwhelmed with feelings that are getting in the way of your understanding of your child, it is essential that you find a support for yourself. You are your child's best support, and the best way to give your child support may well be to find help for yourself.

Being clear about who is responsible

It is important that a protecting parent conveys to the child that it is the perpetrating adult who is responsible for the sexual abuse. Regardless of the child's behaviour, it is an adult's responsibility *not* to sexually abuse. With young children this is easier, but with older girls, adults, including non-abusing parents, can become more confused, mistakenly apportioning blame between the child and the perpetrator. This is often due to the fact that many people view sexualised behaviour as triggering the sexual abuse rather than understanding that such behaviour in children is in fact a *consequence* of being sexually abused (see Chapter 5).

Non-abusing parents can also apportion some blame to themselves: 'If only I had done this, or noticed that . . .' But with hindsight, we are all better protectors. Sexual abuse is maintained by secrecy and plays both on people's naïvety and on the ambiguity of physical contact and public closeness between the perpetrator and his target child.

There are many and complex reasons why sexual abuse is not detected or suspicions not acted on. If it happens, it is not your fault, or the child's, and there is nothing to be gained by blaming yourself. You may want to talk with other adults about why you think you are partly to blame, but your child needs you to be clear that the abuser is responsible for what he did.

What you need

Many of the things your child needs, you will need as well. You may need some distance from the perpetrator, especially if he is your partner. You will need friends and relatives to believe and support you through this experience, and not just in the short term. The pain and upset may feel keenest immediately after the shock has worn off, but often you can still be struggling with the issues and the consequences for you and your children years later.

Give yourself time and space

Having the time and space to work through the feelings brought up by a disclosure of sexual abuse is absolutely vital. For mothers there will be a mixture of conflicting feelings, especially if the perpetrator was also a partner. The feelings regarding your lover or partner need to be dealt with separately from those you have as a parent.

Don't be too quick to decide that everything has been sorted out. Remember, children often disclose in stages, so there may be more to come. Sometimes other children in the family cannot disclose until the abuser has moved out. Whilst a perpetrator's denial may make it hard to believe your child, sometimes an admission lulls a protecting parent into thinking everything will now be all right. Having time with your child but without the abuser is crucial for both of you. You need to be able to respond to your child and think about what you want to do.

Sexual offenders will bring pressure to bear on both the child and their protector to keep quiet about the sexual abuse. So once you have managed to physically distance yourself and your child from the perpetrator, it is essential that you talk to someone about what has happened. Keeping the abuse secret only protects the abuser. He needs to know that you will not hesitate to go outside the immediate family for help and advice and that he needs to do some work on his problem before he can return, if this is something you are considering. If you feel certain your child has been sexually abused, then before considering any return home you should ensure that you and your child feel safe and ready to resume the relationship, and that he admits to the abuse and is prepared to get professional help for his problem.

Even with professional help, it can be several years before everyone is ready to try and live together again. You may decide during that time that you don't want to live together any more. But it is realistic to think in terms of eighteen months to two years before things seem normal again. So be generous with your time for yourself. Don't let anyone rush you into making a decision about the family's future until *you* are ready. Be sure to talk with other supportive and trusted adults before you make any decisions. You should also be confident that your child is beginning to recover from the experience of sexual abuse and that you have helped them in that process. This will offer greater protection in the future, as living with a known sex offender requires the highest levels of monitoring and vigilance on the part of the protecting parent.

Getting support for yourself

There are lots of issues you will need to talk about. This exploration should not be something you do on your own. Other members of the extended family will be confronted with similar feelings of shock and possible disbelief. But their knowledge of everyone involved, coupled with their slight distance from the situation, may make it easier for them to be helpful. Their support is essential to break down the isolation and devastation so many mothers feel following the discovery of sexual abuse.

Although the immediate impulse is to keep it quiet, finding people you can trust to talk to about the abuse is just as important for you as it is for the child. You will need someone who believes and will not judge you, but who will also be honest about the risks involved; someone who will help in practical ways, such as taking the children off your hands for a while, or giving you the space to moan or complain about the situation.

Discovering sexual abuse within your family means you have to be a parent first, putting to one side your healthy adult need for love and affection. Many mothers find that by concentrating on being strong for their children and being a parent first, they manage to cope with the situation better in the short term.[3]

> If you feel *you* are not getting the support or help *you* need, just believe in your own feelings and fight for your child alone, no matter what.
>
> (Kiera)

It is important that the support you seek is selective. In a crisis you can be very vulnerable and needy. In such a state you may talk to everyone about what is happening (although keeping quiet about it is more usual). However talking indiscriminately could jeopardise your child's confidentiality in the wider community. Many people still do not understand sexual abuse, and will make unkind and insensitive remarks both to children who have been sexually abused and to parents. Many non-abusing parents turn to professionals for help and support. This may involve your child's teacher, your GP or health visitor, or the child protection agencies. Statutory agencies should be a resource and support for non-abusing parents. Getting the best from them is discussed in detail in Chapter 7.

In many places there are groups for parents whose children have been sexually abused. These can be a very useful source of support as the other parents will be going through, or may have gone through, the same things as you are.

> The group has helped me face really hard times by letting me know that I am not the only mother going through hell because my children were abused . . .[4]

Sometimes local women's centres, Citizens' Advice Bureaux, phone lines, women's refuges and **Rape Crisis Centres** can give you information and suggestions about where you can get help and support.

The increased monitoring a vulnerable child needs when sexual abuse has taken place is best carried out by someone who knows the child well, who cares for and loves the child, and whom the child can trust. These protectors usually come from within the child's nuclear and extended family. Social workers, by virtue of the demands on their professional time, will offer only a minimum level of protection. Teachers have to spread their professional attention across a number of children. This is why it is important for you to be able to talk about the sexual abuse, not only with professionals but also with your family, friends and wider network.

Talking about it with family

It is important for the other children in the family to be given some information about what has happened, especially if it results in the removal of either the child who has disclosed or the perpetrator. They need to know in age-appropriate language what has been disclosed. For young children this can be minimal but still clearly convey important information that, for example, 'Daddy has had to leave home because he did something wrong. He touched Sally in a way he should not have.' Children may ask questions that do not have immediate answers, such as 'When will he be back?' It is important that you are honest with them. It is better to say you do not know than to make up something.

If a parent who is the subject of an allegation moves out while the allegation is being investigated, it may be more helpful to be vague about the concerns until the investigation has been completed. For example, 'Daddy may have done something he shouldn't have.' If children indicate they know something more specific, it signals to the protecting parent that a more detailed response is required.

Children's requests for information about experiences of

sexual abuse often occur at different developmental stages. This is equally true of requests for information from non-abused siblings. They may, when they are much older, ask for more specific information that may have led to a dramatic change in their family's life.

Child sexual abuse encourages both adults and children to keep secrets. It is not easy to start talking openly and honestly about something which has been kept a secret for so long. The feelings of guilt on the part of both parent and child can be very strong, and can make it extremely difficult to explore some issues in depth.

> [My sister] has been asking like, who her – who her dad is ... And, me and my mum, we just both look at one another and sort of, like, think. My mum said that my sister's just gonna think he's dead. If she wanna know, somehow she'll find out. I'm just wondering how she's gonna react when she finds out ... If she finds out ... she'll wonder why we didn't tell her ...
>
> (Alison)

In these families, younger siblings may well want to know at a later stage why Daddy no longer lives with them or sees them any more.

It can be useful to have someone outside the family to help you talk about the sexual abuse with your children.

> It needs to be highlighted that parents need help on how to speak to the child after abuse. My knowledge of this was very little ... Once there's more help for the parent, then of course it must help the child and be less stressful.
>
> (Kiera)

Sometimes being with other mothers who have been through the same experience is a first step to being able to talk about it at all.

Do you feel you are the only parent going through hell? Do you think you have been branded as a bad person walking about with a label pinned on you saying your children were sexually abused? ... Don't try to take all the blame for what happened ... It is a great help to know you are not the only one, as I thought.[5]

When involving members of your extended family, it is important to pick someone you trust and on whom you can rely. Kiera's sister and mother were especially supportive and were able to help her deal with her partner's sexual offending.

Involving friends and community

Just as you need to choose who to talk to in your wider family, you need to be selective with regard to your friends and those in the wider community. You may also need to help your child with this by identifying who outside the immediate family they can talk to about the sexual abuse. Whomever you choose needs to believe it has happened and be discreet, as it is important to protect your child from ignorant comments and prurient interest. Your child needs to know who knows what about them and their experience of sexual abuse.

Many women and children from minority ethnic communities feel they will not be supported by their community if they disclose sexual abuse from within the community.[6] They often feel a conflict of loyalties because most outside child protection agencies do not represent the interests of their communities and have a history of intervening inappropriately.[7]

So it is extremely important within minority ethnic communities that child protection as an issue is taken seriously by the community. This will convey to the child and any protecting parent that support and resources are available from within the community.

Statutory child protection agencies operate within the dominant language – English. In a multi-lingual family the potential protector may not speak the dominant language. Access to English may be controlled by the perpetrator, thus restricting the options of both the target and the possible protector. In such instances, it is essential that the non-abusing parent get help from someone within their community.

It is easier for all communities to think of sexual abuse as something perpetrated by an outsider. Yet it is all too clear that sexual offences against children are most likely to be perpetrated by someone known to the child. This is true for all communities. However for minority ethnic communities, child protection also involves protecting your children from racist attacks which are clearly perpetrated by individuals who are not members of the minority ethnic community. But it is important that protecting the community from outsiders does not lead to a denial that anything negative, including sexual abuse by members of the community, can happen. A denial that it happens silences the survivors within any community and often presents them with what should be an unnecessary choice – belonging in silence, or speaking out and finding there is no place within the community for their reality. This would have a very negative impact on the child's recovery process and the community would then become a refuge for those who inflict damage on its own members. By tackling issues of child protection, communities make themselves strong enough to both confront sexual offenders and facilitate the recovery of those who have been offended against.

Blocks to being an effective protector

Sometimes there will be factors that get in the way of being an effective protector.

Not believing

Not believing your child is the biggest block to being an effective protector. If you are finding it really hard to believe what your child has said or what others are telling you has happened, it can be helpful to talk about this with someone else. Try and sort out which bits you are struggling with.

You may need to think about what would help you believe or be convinced it has happened. Remember, admissions by abusers are rare. There is often no medical evidence, no police charges and no conviction. Listen to what your child has said to you or to other people.

If you believe your child has been sexually abused but not by the person they have named, tell them you believe they have been sexually abused and you want to make sure it does not happen again.

If you continue to disbelieve your child you will be hurting them and it is likely the abuser will continue with the abuse. The child can also think that you *know* it is happening even though you *say* you don't believe them. Perfectly adequate protection plans can be devised without knowing who has sexually abused the child.

Vulnerabilities

Sexual offenders can target women or children who have vulnerabilities, such as a physical or intellectual disability. This is precisely because they can increase the woman or child's dependency on them. Such vulnerabilities can also make it more difficult to be an effective protector because it may be harder to access outside sources of support. In some cases, the perpetrator may accentuate the disability and increase the dependency purposefully.

Disabilities which may increase the vulnerabilities of an individual, and impact negatively on their capacity to protect not only themselves but also their children, include communication difficulties such as deafness, where oral communication may be limited, or the use of sign language as 'mother tongue', and physical disabilities that restrict the mobility of a possible protector. The freedom of movement a potential protector would need could be severely curtailed and controlled by someone who wished to increase the physical dependency that is already present.

To reduce these vulnerabilities, potential protectors must have access to an outside source of support that would be able to help if sexual abuse was an issue. There are frequently outside support groups to which women can go, but unless the support group has already considered the issue of child sexual abuse, then the response may not be appropriate or helpful. Group members may be too shocked to help; they may disbelieve the woman or blame her for what has happened; they may ostracise her, thereby increasing her isolation and possible dependency on the perpetrator; they may feel too uncomfortable even to discuss the issue. Some members of the group may not have children themselves, and so thinking about protection and parenting might not be something they have begun to address.

It is important for all protecting adults, including those with disabilities, to identify and establish a network or potential support group for themselves by raising sexual abuse as an issue in their current group. It is becoming increasingly clear that sexual offenders not only target women whom they perceive as being vulnerable, but will also target children with disabilities who may be less able to protect themselves from sexual abuse. Any vulnerable member of the community can be targeted for a whole range of abuses, including sexual abuse.

Vulnerabilities such as a physical or intellectual disability are not necessarily a block to effective protection, but it is useful to develop protective strategies for yourself and your child.

Survivors and parenting

Many people believe that having a history of sexual abuse yourself will impact negatively on your capacity to protect. In the majority of cases this is unlikely to be true, as often those people who have experienced victimisation or discrimination are the quickest to recognise abusive situations.

If you have been sexually abused as a child, you may be more sensitive to the signs or indicators that your child is being sexually abused. You may be more able to believe a child's disclosure, and convey that belief to the child unequivocally. But if you have been sexually abused and never disclosed this information or talked about it to anyone, discovering that your child has also been subjected to this experience can be very disturbing to you personally because it may activate traumatic material that you had managed to 'put away'.

Working on your own experiences of sexual abuse following the discovery that your child, too, has been a victim is possibly not the ideal time. Recovery work in sexual abuse often makes you feel helpless and like a child. This feeling would be incompatible with what your child needs from you at this point – a parent who believes and who can help them to recover. The last thing a child needs is to sense that you are feeling especially vulnerable. Children who have been sexually abused are often very sensitive to adults' needs, and if they sense that their experience disturbs you they may choose not to talk to you about it.

So, if you decide that this new disclosure has brought up unresolved feelings for you about your childhood experience, it may be helpful for you to find someone to help you talk through your feelings. It is important, though, for your child's recovery that you remain a parent to them; that you are clear it is not their fault that you are remembering things you would rather not; and that you are not angry with them for disclosing the current abuse.

Ongoing abuse

If a potential protector is still being sexually abused by her childhood perpetrator, or currently being physically and/or sexually abused by her partner, it will be extremely difficult for her to be an effective protector for her children. She should take immediate steps to protect herself from the abuse, and check that the child is not at risk from the violence she is experiencing.[8]

Violence, which can seem so personal, is likely in fact to be more generalised, and the violent man may well be attacking more than one individual. Women leaving violent and abusive partners may think their children are better off remaining, and that the violence and abuse will now stop. This is unlikely to be true.

Domestic violence between parents seriously compromises

the protective capacities of both parents. Children can be frightened to let possible protectors know about sexual abuse for fear of the repercussions, both for themselves and for possible protectors. If children witness their father beating their mother, and they themselves are subjected to his physical, as well as sexual, violence, it is most unlikely they will perceive their mother as someone who could protect them. They are more likely to perceive her as a victim like themselves. Establishing parental authority in situations like this can be very difficult and demoralising for the non-abusing parent.

Violence encourages children to be passive and submit or to become violent themselves. It is likely that, rather than learning to protect themselves and others from physical and sexual violence, children who witness violence in their immediate surroundings are at best learning to live with it; at worst they are learning to do it themselves.

Clearly it is not possible to begin recovery work in such a hostile environment. The safety of both the child and the possible protector must be secured first.

Maintaining the Context for Recovery

It may be easier to see the importance of some of the issues that have been raised in the short term, but it is important to continue to keep protection to the forefront in your family and your community. This will help to reduce the risk of revictimisation and will encourage everyone to take personal safety seriously. As your child grows up it is appropriate for them to take on some responsibility for their own safety. Teaching them to be assertive, to be clear about what they like and don't like, to talk to someone if they are confused, to let you know where they are going, with whom and for how long, are all part of developing self-protection skills. If other adults in your network are also giving these messages to children, the positive impact will be that much greater. For those children who have already been sexually abused, their recovery work will be facilitated by a more receptive wider community that can deal with any unresolved issues as and when they arise. So it is vital to establish a wider context for recovery within which any child and any one possible protector can begin to recover from an experience of sexual abuse.

A readiness to believe child sexual abuse happens prior to a specific incident makes it more likely that the potential protector and their children can remain connected to their community. In communities where sexual abuse is considered impossible, a disclosure which challenges that belief often produces ostracism, not for the perpetrator of the sexual abuse, who frequently accesses privileged status by virtue of gender or class, but for the child who discloses, and sometimes the parent who tries to protect. Raising the issue of child sexual abuse before it happens will empower future protectors and encourage children to tell if they are being sexually abused.

To be an effective protector it is essential that you have access to other adults who support and affirm your authority within the family. It is also important that there is a place for you to take your feelings of guilt, shame, anger, sadness and betrayal, which at the same time recognises the continuing parental tasks you still have to provide. You will probably need a separate forum to deal with personal feelings that will be making it more difficult to help your children begin to recover from the experience of sexual abuse.

Establishing a context for recovery is not the sole responsibility of a non-abusing parent. It needs to be much wider – a responsibility embraced by the whole adult community. This will not only help protect all the children of the community, but also make it easier for those who do experience sexual abuse to tell, and to begin their recovery process. A believing, supportive response from a protecting parent is clearly that much more potent if the same protective and corrective messages are echoed by the wider community: You are not alone. It is not your fault. It should not have happened. We are sorry that it did happen. You were right to tell, and together we are going to get over it.

CHAPTER FIVE

The Emotional Consequences of Sexual Abuse

This chapter outlines some of the effects of sexual abuse to help protecting adults understand what the child may be feeling. This understanding should enable you to be more helpful to the child concerned and suggest areas to focus on in the recovery process.

Research on the consequences of sexual abuse makes it clear that many types of psychological problem can be caused by, or are related to, the experience of sexual abuse.

The traumatic effects of sexual abuse are affected by a number of factors. These include the age at which it started, how long it went on, the relationship of the perpetrator to the child, if and how the sexual abuse was stopped, and perhaps most significantly, the support the child received once it had been discovered. Clearly if the abuse is short-lived, terminated by effective action by the child and/or a non-abusing parent or sibling, and the child is supported and believed by their immediate network, then the negative consequences will be minimised. Belief by a protecting adult, preferably a parental figure, is the single best predictor for a good recovery.

If a child is not believed, they usually have to put up with the sexual abuse and learn to live with it. Roland Summit called this process of learning to live with the reality of sexual abuse 'accommodation'.[1] When a child is trying to cope with the abuse in this way, the trauma they are experiencing often manifests itself as challenging behaviour. And while that behaviour may seem dysfunctional to an outsider it may be uniquely functional for the child.

Ironically, over time it is often the challenging behaviour that becomes identified as the problem rather than the sexual abuse which is the cause of it. Once the possible cause of the behaviour is discovered, however, this does not lead to 'symptomatic' behaviour miraculously disappearing. The behaviour used to accommodate the sexual abuse will have become a habitual way of behaving.

All, well most of these times I was drunk ... Even now when I am pissed off or I can't handle what is going on, I think of drinking. A few months ago I went through a phase of waking up and drinking, coming home and drinking. Once I took some vodka into school and drank it during the day. I had a supply of vodka and Malibu at home. It just got my mind off the thing which was upsetting me.

(Lisa)

Sexual abuse necessarily involves emotional abuse and physical abuse. Categories of risk used by child protection agencies imply that sexual, physical and emotional abuse are separate and distinct from one another. But it may be more useful to see the categories escalating where each successive category includes the one before. Sexual abuse is emotionally abusive because of the distorted and perverted relationship created by the sexual offender to facilitate the abuse. It is physical abuse, even though it may not result in physical injuries, because it is a colonisation of the child's body. The natural discovery and pleasure in the physical self is interfered with for the gratification of someone else.

Child sexual abuse impacts on all areas of development. It cannot be recommended as an experience and protecting adults need to be working towards creating communities which value and respect everyone, including children. The negative consequences of sexual abuse are becoming increasingly apparent as more adults speak of their own experiences and protection agencies become more active in uncovering sexual abuse for a younger generation of survivors.

However, because research has not been done to follow up people who have been sexually abused in childhood but do not use the mental health system as adults, it can be easy to assume that all victims of sexual abuse will experience devastating psychological consequences. This is probably not the case for a number of survivors; some people are able to recover from their experiences of childhood sexual abuse without professional help or intervention. This should encourage non-abusing adults in adopting a more proactive, protective stance. It is very likely that the silent survivors who have made positive recoveries from the early childhood trauma of sexual abuse have met with sympathetic and helpful responses from those around them.

Understanding both the long- and short-term consequences of sexual abuse will help non-abusing parents and other adults facilitate the recovery of any child who has been sexually abused who confides in them.

In the short term, immediately following disclosure of sexual abuse, the child often experiences an increase in feelings of fear, depression, anger, hostility and aggression.[2] Since many sexual offenders will have used a combination of threats and bribes to secure the child's silence and compliance, the child will probably be frightened and anxious after disclosing. This is why the child's safety and the distance between the child and the perpetrator are emphasised in Chapter 4, which discusses establishing and maintaining a context for recovery. Knowing the specific threats the perpetrator used is important because protectors can then reassure the child that these threats will not materialise.

> ... he used to say I'd be taken into care if I ever told. My mum would just put me away ... or they'd take me away from my mum.
>
> (Alison)

If the abuse goes on, or if the child's concerns and emotional distress are not addressed, then the child's feelings of anger, hostility, depression and aggression will become exacerbated and potentially more disruptive.

I get really angry towards myself because I think what happened was my fault and because I think I should have stopped it; also the fact that although I was drunk, I let so many things happen; also because of things that happened when I was sober but honestly I just did it to stop it going on and to keep him quiet, to stop giving me hassles.

(Lisa)

Self-destructive behaviour; high levels of anxiety; isolation and stigmatisation; low self-esteem or self-esteem derived from sexual activities alone; difficulties in forming trusting and safe relationships; revictimsation and further exploitation; substance and alcohol abuse; and possible sexual maladjustment can all follow.[3]

Some children exhibit all of these difficulties. The majority will have some difficulties in specific areas. In a small proportion of cases, the child will show no outward signs of distress and be able to get on with age-appropriate tasks.

Areas of concern

This section focuses on specific aspects of the child's development that may be distorted by an experience of sexual abuse. As a protecting adult, you need to be giving the child the knowledge and experience of interacting with a non-abusing adult. This should help to correct some of the distortions, and facilitate the child's recovery process.

Developing an appropriate body image and healthy self-esteem

Most children develop a sense of personal space at a young age. This includes a basic understanding of 'where my body begins and ends'. For a child who is sexually abused from infancy this fundamental concept of separateness and the establishment of an appropriate body image is interfered with. The child can become intrusive and show no understanding of privacy or personal space. Their touching is often over-familiar and their need for close physical contact overwhelming. This physical contact is often highly sexualised, and adult recipients experience intense discomfort when approached. This can lead adults who come in contact with the child to be physically rejecting at a time when the child's need for physical reassurance is likely to be great.

The child may need to be taught how to give and receive non-sexual physical affection. They will need to be reminded about personal space and praised when they begin to assert their own need for privacy and personal space as well as respecting that of others.

Not all children are sexualised by the experience of sexual abuse. More commonly the child feels used and dirty. They can feel insignificant, especially if no one has noticed they were being sexually abused. Taking the time to ask and to be concerned directly challenges the child's belief that they are of no worth or value. They can neglect themselves and not attend to their most basic physical needs; or they can become disconnected from the messages their body is giving them, such as 'I am hungry' or 'I am no longer hungry'. The invisibility they feel can be matched by their appearance, as is the case with severe anorexics, or be totally at odds with their physical size or presence. One young woman who shouted all the time when she spoke said she had to speak so loud or she would not be heard. So the distortion of body image and body messages can be extremely profound and sometimes not based on reality. Only constant feedback from protecting adults can begin to change this perception: 'I can see you. I can hear. I do believe you exist.'

Many children who have been sexually abused feel as if they have been profoundly and irreversibly damaged by the experience. Suzanne Sgroi refers to this as the 'damaged goods syndrome'.[4] Alternatively, some children will come to perceive their self-worth only in terms of their usefulness as a sex object. This can lead to the child relating to the world through sexual activity of one kind or another, sometimes almost exclusively. Some children will need help controlling the strong sexual feelings that have been triggered by the inappropriate sexual contact. They have developmentally inappropriate sexual knowledge which cannot be taken from them. It may be important to correct sexual misinformation they may have acquired, as well as providing an appropriate context for them to explore their bodies.

The child may be used to an audience and be very insistent on involving others (both adults and children) in sexual interactions. The child needs to be given alternative ways of interacting by protecting adults. For example, if a child tries to give an adult an open-mouthed kiss, a protecting adult can say, 'No, children and adults don't kiss that way. This is how they give each other kisses', and then follow up with a clear, unambiguous kiss on the cheek.

Protecting adults need to ensure that any sexual behaviour the child is manifesting is contained in a private place, such as the child's bedroom. It may also be necessary to ensure they are not hurting themselves when they are being sexual. Many children who have been sexually abused and who are showing very sexualised behaviour can be hurting themselves when they masturbate, either through their own rough handling or by inserting objects into their genitals and bottoms.

The sexualisation described above is not an amplification of normal childhood sensuality. Sexual feelings for the child are likely to be overwhelming and grossly distorted. The child will lack the cognitive skills to understand what is happening to their bodies and over time may become addicted to the heightened physiological state the sexual abuse produces – in some cases a potent combination of both fear and sexual arousal.

Developing a positive self-image
In considering the impact of sexual abuse on the development of a positive self-image, it is important to consider the wider social influences on this process for all children. There are very powerful messages about gender and race that impact on the formation of a positive self-image. Not all of these messages are positive but clearly significant adults in a child's

life can counteract to some effect those messages that encourage a child to feel negatively about aspects of themselves.

It is important to consider how sexual abuse will impact on a child's understanding of self. For boys who have been sexually abused by men, the issue of becoming a man can be problematic. Unless a boy who has been sexually abused by a man has access to other non-abusing males, he may assume that all males become perpetrators as they become men. If he does not want to follow this perceived pattern, his identification as a male is in jeopardy.

A boy sexually abused by a man may want to convince himself that he has not been damaged by what would be considered by many to be a homosexual encounter, and he might then become deliberately sexually aggressive towards women. A boy abused by a man will have to deal with wider society's homophobia as the shared gender of child and perpetrator often becomes the focus rather than the adult sexual exploitation of the child. Fears about issues relating to homosexuality are thought to be one of the main reasons boys are reluctant to disclose sexual abuse by men, despite the fact that many male perpetrators who target boys also target girls and women and would describe themselves as heterosexual.

For black children, dominant racist perspectives of black and minority ethnic sexuality will impact on the child's experience, especially if the sexual abuse is disclosed to someone from outside the community. The child might not want to disclose under these circumstances, or alternatively these views may confirm the child's own limited experience of the community. Black men can be portrayed as sexually voracious; black girls as sexually precocious; black women as sexually promiscuous; Asian men as sexually repressed; Asian women as sexually exotic. There are numerous stereotypes combining sexuality, race and culture promoted by dominant groups. There will also be sexual stereotypes promoted within minority ethnic communities that the dominant group is not aware of.

However, sexual offenders as a group will employ any stereotype that facilitates the sexual abuse and serves to rationalise their behaviour. The child is unlikely to know this and may believe the stereotypes to be truly representative of a particular gender or race. In this way their identity can be profoundly damaged as they may try to reject aspects of themselves that they associate negatively with their experience of sexual abuse.

Learning to have and express feelings appropriately

Children who are sexually abused live in an internal world of secrecy and confusion. This can make it difficult for them to express a whole range of different emotions and feelings, and leads to a very restricted affective range. They are allowed, or allow themselves, to express only certain feelings. Much of the anger they feel when being sexually abused must be repressed (they are not aware of it) or suppressed (they are aware of it but are not free to express it directly).

> Often I don't know how to express my feelings ... and I become frustrated and depressed. I am also moody and very sarcastic on the subject of life. That is when I want to cut myself or run away because I don't know how to express myself.
>
> (Lisa)

Anxiety, fear and depression may be overwhelming but they are often disguised either as unrelenting hyperactivity or under a flat, unexpressive exterior. Many adults diagnosed as suffering from post-traumatic stress disorder[5] exhibit what is called a numbed responsiveness to the outside world. Sometimes this can be seen in children as well.

Keeping such powerful feelings in check all of the time is extremely difficult. Sometimes there will be dramatic, explosive outbursts. This can include suicide attempts or violent attacks on others.

> If I get in an argument with someone, I think back and I start building up a hate for that person, and like, bringing

all the blame down on that person. Sometimes I get pretty violent because of it.

(Alison)

I would love to punch him until there was no more energy in me and he could feel the anger inside me. Sometimes I feel so angry I just want to hurt myself but I don't . . . and I'm confused and I just have so much tension inside of me and I pace round the room thinking of things that I could do to myself even though I don't really want to. I need to release the anger in me but I can't. I hate myself and feel ugly and dirty for doing what he wanted. I can't stand myself.

(Lisa)

Many children who have been sexually abused do not feel entitled to any feelings at all. Given that their feelings have been ignored by the perpetrator, and misinterpreted or not recognised by a possible protector or protectors, this is not surprising. Additionally, children and young people who have been sexually abused are likely to receive strong messages from others regarding what they should feel about their experience. Rather than being allowed to discover their own feelings, they can have other people's feelings and expectations about how they should feel pushed on to them. This can range from an expectation that they should be angry when they may not be, to pressure to get over it when they are not yet ready to do so.

It is important that the recovery process helps the child or young person learn to recognise and identify their feelings and then to express them appropriately. This can take a long time, and can involve a whole range of experiences, possibly including therapeutic work.

[To begin] everyone [in my group] was, like . . . isolated from everyone else. We were just sort of sat there, and none of us wanted to talk about it.

Some of the girls [in my group] were pretty angry – you

couldn't get straight talk out of them. They'd just say, like, they wanted to kill him . . .

[The group] helped us get out some of the anger that we had bottled up inside.

[In family sessions with Mum] it was good to be next to her to hear what she was feeling.

(Alison)

Sexual abuse severely restricts the range of emotions and feelings that can be expressed not only by the child but also by others within the immediate family.

Support and a safe context to explore feelings are an essential part of the recovery process for everyone involved. Support for child and care giver is essential.

I have my own feelings on the abuse and haven't made her feel the same as myself . . . I have tried not to let her see how I feel about the abuse and how I hate her daddy for doing it. I don't want her to have to choose sides . . . I want her to be central right now and maybe when she's older, she will feel different or understand the reasons for my feelings.

(Kiera, Jasmine's mother)

Judging safe people and situations

Children who have been sexually abused by a parent figure have been betrayed. It can be difficult for the child to decide how to judge future relationships when such a primary one has been violated. Children either learn to rely on their personal experience to judge individuals or remain confused and essentially vulnerable to inappropriate relationships because of their inability to judge what or who is safe.

It can be helpful to give children and young people a problem-solving approach to assess people and situations rather than a list of safe places or people. Such an approach encourages children to learn how to judge situations and people, and suggests that they let others know where they are, what they are doing and who with.[6]

It can also be helpful to identify situations that may be risky, especially for adolescents, who quite appropriately should be taking some responsibility for their own personal safety. This can include using drugs or drink where their ability to protect themselves would be negligible; going unaccompanied or with people they don't know to a place they don't know; getting into a car with a driver who is clearly drunk. It may also be important for protecting adults to teach children the assertiveness skills they will need to say no and get away from situations that don't feel comfortable. There are several resources which outline such skills, and details of these are in the appendix at the back of this book.

Developing an appropriate sense of responsibility

Many children who have been sexually abused feel responsible.

> I feel guilty for hating him because I sometimes feel sorry for him thinking that what happened was my fault and because of me he is locked up.
>
> (Lisa)

> I used to think it was all my fault . . . it took a *very* lot of encouraging . . . that it wasn't my fault, it was theirs . . . I always thought I made them do it.
>
> (Natasha)

Q: Who do you think is responsible?
Alison: I've learned this [laughing] – him. I still feel like I should have told sooner – and told him 'No'.
Q: And if you had told him 'No', what do you think he would have done?
Alison: Just done it anyway [laughs].
Q: Because, let's think – you were giving out 'No' signals . . .

Alison: I just used to sort of cringe. I can just remember when he took me out once – he was buying stuff and I was standing there, and I was going 'I don't want it.' I thought if I didn't take nothing off of him, that I wouldn't have to do anything. I can remember saying 'No, I don't want that – no.'

Q: Who do you think your mum thinks is responsible?

Alison: Him – because he's an adult – he should have had more sense.

Q: Do you believe that?

Alison: Sometimes . . .

Q: What do you think it would take for you to stop feeling responsible?

Alison: I don't think I ever will.

Sexual offenders encourage the child to feel responsible as this encourages the child's sense of entrapment that facilitates the continuation of the sexual abuse. The child's sense of responsibility can often become distorted. They can feel overly responsible even for things that are clearly not their responsibility, as in Lisa's case where the judge who gave her abuser a custodial sentence is obviously responsible for his being in jail. Frequently children feel guilty and feel they need to be punished as well. They can inflict the punishment on themselves by self-harming or trying to kill themselves.

If it is the child who is removed from the family home and not the perpetrator, this further complicates the issues, both of who is responsible, and of who is to blame. Failure to believe a child's disclosure, whether on the part of the non-abusing parent or professional child protection agencies, will almost certainly make the child think they are in the wrong, that it is their fault, and that no one believes them. By implication it suggests to the child that sexual abuse did not really happen, that they should not have told about it, and if removal occurs it is because they were wrong to speak out and are being sent away or punished for doing so. Children can also continue to try to protect both the perpetrator and the non-abusing parent by remaining quiet, retracting their allegation, or attempting to make things better by taking over caring for the family.

However, in addition to feeling responsible themselves, many children also locate some of the responsibility with their mothers or the non-abusing parent. Helping a child or young person to understand who is responsible for the sexual abuse is one of the first steps towards helping them to recover. This means being clear that the abuser is responsible for his actions; not the child or the non-abusing adult. As the child matures, they will have to learn to take responsibility for their own behaviour too; and to know that a history of childhood sexual abuse will not excuse them from taking personal responsibility for their actions as they grow older. Protecting adults need to help clarify who is responsible for what, and help the child develop a realistic sense of personal responsibility.

Developing an understanding about right and wrong

Sexual abuse of children is fundamentally tied up with issues of right and wrong which are the cornerstone of moral development. Unfortunately society is equivocal about how wrong sexual abuse is. This is conveyed in a number of ways, not least of which are the mitigating circumstances to be taken into consideration when sentencing a convicted sexual offender.[7] Mitigating factors include a plea of guilt, the father had a genuine affection for his daughter, and/or she has had previous sexual experience. Older girls in particular are often seen as partially responsible for their own sexual abuse. Recently there was an outcry when a judge, sentencing a convicted sexual offender, described the eight-year-old victim as 'no angel'.[8] This kind of statement implies the child has some responsibility for the sexual abuse. Legally this is construed as contributory negligence. This concept is frequently used in rape and domestic violence cases where the actions of the women are seen as contributing to the commission of the crime.

In the absence of a clear statement that sexual abuse is

wrong, and the supporting of that statement of belief by everyone that the child will come into contact with, that is, society at large, it may be difficult for children who have been sexually abused to develop the necessary repugnance to sexual abuse that prevents the crossover from victim to perpetrator that occurs for some children.

Juvenile sexual offending is extremely serious, and perhaps more common than previously thought. However it is often minimised, not only by the juveniles, usually male, who are involved, but also by their parents and sometimes by child protection agencies as well. The consequences for the child who is targeted or victimised are often just as devastating as if the offender were an adult. The consequences will be worse if the activities are not identified as sexual abuse and no protective measures are taken.

The minimisation of the impact of juvenile sexual offending and younger children's sexual bullying is unfortunate as there is good reason to believe that, dealt with effectively at a young age, the likelihood of further sexual offending can be significantly reduced.[9]

Protecting adults must convey clear messages about the rights and wrongs of sexual abuse. This should make it clearer that the *action* itself is wrong, not the getting caught. Children need protective adults to be clear that sexual abuse is wrong; that, while there may be many explanations for the sexual abuse, there are no excuses; and that protecting adults have a responsibility to prevent it from happening. These statements can be made regardless of the outcome of a case of sexual abuse. In Alison's case, for example, the perpetrator was acquitted on a legal technicality. This did not change Alison's mother's mind about what happened, nor any of the workers involved in supporting Alison. The damaging consequences of the acquittal were reduced by the clear position protecting adults maintained.

Developing positive relationships

Sexual abuse impacts on a child's capacity to make and sustain relationships. Closeness and intimacy may seem threatening. Adults as protectors may seem an alien concept.

Many young people who have been sexually abused do not know how to negotiate relationships, especially non-sexual ones. They can exchange one abusive relationship for another. They can also be very dependent, almost unable to function on their own. This is due to the low self-esteem, guilt and confusion they can feel about the sexual abuse. The secrecy surrounding the sexual abuse may also have made it difficult to think of establishing independent relationships outside the family. Alternatively, the child may be pushed prematurely into other intimate relationships.

> It affected me in going out with boys, 'cause, like, everyone was going out with boys and I was thinking 'I AM NOT going out with a boy.' It took me until I was, like, nine or ten to really go out with a boy properly. And I thought, 'Alright, this is alright. Now what's the next step?'
>
> (Natasha)

A child may be distrustful of adults and may be overly reliant on peer relationships. This may be quite functional as good friends can help the recovery process begin. However, if the young person's relationships are sexualised, then there is an increased risk that they may be exploited sexually again. A high degree of dependency makes them very vulnerable and easily targeted by other sexual offenders who can exploit the healthy need for a relationship to their own ends. Pimps will use this tactic in breaking in young girls and boys to prostitution. They often 'rescue' the child from an abusive situation. They spend time listening, taking care of the child, and offer gifts, ranging from a place to stay, to food, money, drugs or drink – all of which increase the child's dependency on them. They can then exploit this dependency by asking, often forcing, the child to repay the kindness.

A child may decide to avoid all relationships as being too risky. They may try to take care of all of their own needs and will make only superficial relationships with people, avoiding any intimacy.

Protecting adults need to prepare themselves for the distrust and rejection they will experience when trying to renegotiate or begin a relationship with a child who has been sexually abused. Appropriate adult–child relationships will have been eclipsed by the inappropriate relationship between a sexual offender and his target.

It is also important to encourage appropriate peer relationships, especially same-sex friends. There is enormous pressure on young people to be involved in romantic relationships without recognising all the complexities and complications that may exist, especially for someone who has a history of childhood sexual abuse.

Talking about an experience of sexual abuse within the context of a safe, trusting relationship that does not involve sexual intimacy, such as with a parent, friend or professional helper, is the most important part of the recovery process. This will enable the child to develop their own sense of self-worth as a person and give them the best possible basis from which to explore intimate relationships with partners.

Developing a positive sexual identity

Sexual abuse can distort an individual's sexual development. The child may have been given misinformation about sex by the perpetrator, or may have made incorrect inferences themselves as a consequence of early developmentally inappropriate sexual contact. They can be unclear about reproduction, or believe that their internal organs have been damaged by the experience.

The child or young person will need information on sex, biology and reproduction. It will be difficult for them to make best use of the sex education that is offered in school because it will be hard for them to judge what is developmentally appropriate knowledge. To ask any questions might indicate to peers that something has happened. So it can be helpful to provide some idea about what other children of a similar age might know. Often these misperceptions may not be evident until adolescence, when it is developmentally appropriate for a younger person to want to establish more intimate relationships.

However, many young people who have been sexually abused find it difficult to share their history of sexual abuse with prospective sexual partners. They worry that it will be used against them, or that it will turn their partners from them. Sometimes they feel they do not know their partners well enough to share this part of their life. But consensual sexual activity can unintentionally trigger memories of the original sexual abuse, and this can lead to a variety of consequences such as distress during sex, avoidance of sexual intimacy or withdrawing from sexual activity during sex. This is further compounded by having then to deal with the partner's disappointment, upset and/or confusion over what has happened.

Having a flashback to a sexually abusive experience whilst having sex with a partner is extremely unpleasant. If it is not shared, then the consensual sexual intimacy can become perverted, possibly by making a consensual experience a re-creation of the original sexual abuse. It can also reactivate the issue of secrecy. Hopefully a sensitive partner will pick up the non-verbal signs that indicate something is wrong, and will feel confident and concerned enough to ask why. With young people, this requires a high level of maturity.

Children who have experienced sexual abuse can be sexually stimulated and become accustomed to the feeling of being sexually aroused most of the time. In a sexually abusive household this can be functional. However, when they are no longer being sexually abused children can still be left with strong feelings of arousal and not know what to do other than make inappropriate sexual overtures to others, or masturbate.

Many young women who have been sexually abused continue to have sexual relationships with men, sometimes compulsively. This is often not perceived as being problematic, because it represents a socially accepted expression of sexuality. But the compulsive quality is indicative of the distress and confusion the young woman bears, and is likely to increase her vulnerability to a whole host of risks. Teaching young people to be protectively discriminating about sexual partners is especially important if they have also experienced sexual abuse. They can mistakenly assume that high levels of sexual activity demonstrate that they have not been damaged sexually by the abusive experience. It is also likely that they will have learned to 'turn themselves off' to avoid feeling or even thinking about their past experience, especially during sexual activity, which often triggers the unwanted memories or sensations.

Homosexuality is often seen as a negative outcome of sexual abuse, and equated with damaged sexuality. But compulsive and indiscriminate heterosexuality may be a consequence for girl children sexually abused by men, and, in this case, homosexuality for the young woman might be a more positive way for her to continue exploring her sexuality with fewer triggers to traumatic material. For boy children sexually abused by men, there can be a fear that having had this experience means they are homosexual. In this case, it is important to stress the importance of choice in sexual orientation.

Being sexually abused by someone of the same sex does not 'make' someone homosexual. Being sexually aroused by someone of the same sex in the context of being sexually abused does not mean the experience was really wanted or that secretly the victim is homosexual. These issues need to be raised sensitively when helping children and young people who have been sexually abused by someone of the same sex.

It is also necessary to recognise that the wider social context condones and encourages heterosexuality. This wider social acceptance of heterosexuality often leads to heterosexual sexual abuse which involves either adult male sexual abuse of girls or adult female sexual abuse of boys being minimised and not taken seriously. In contrast, homosexual sexual abuse which involves adult male sexual abuse of boys is frequently seen as being more perverted than heterosexual sexual abuse. Adult female sexual abuse of girls is often not even considered. These attitudes reflect wider societal views regarding sexuality and sexual orientation; it may be necessary to challenge these views in order to help a child recover from *any* sexually abusive experience. What is most important is for the child or young person to feel positive about the sexual choices they have made, and comfortable with their own identity as a sexual being.

It is also important to consider that for some children or young people it may not be possible to reclaim their sexual identity as it is so powerfully connected to their experience of sexual abuse. Their feelings about their sexuality and their desire to share this aspect of themselves with someone else may change over time. A period of celibacy may be extremely helpful and a lifetime of celibacy may well be a constructive resolution.

High levels of sexual activity, coupled with an early childhood experience of sexual abuse, increases the risk for a host of health problems, including cervical cancer, fertility problems, and sexually transmitted diseases including HIV and AIDS. Protecting adults will need to raise these kinds of issues more explicitly and almost certainly well in advance of when you would for a child who had not been sexually abused. They are unlikely to raise these issues with you – or with their sexual partner – and will need a protecting adult to take the lead either by discussing or providing written materials that might help (see the resources in the appendix).

Developing good communication skills

Living with sexual abuse creates an atmosphere of secrecy in the family. Communications cannot be trusted as the child can never be sure what they mean. The child who is being sexually abused can be hyperattentive, waiting and watching for the signs that might indicate another episode of sexual abuse is about to happen. This, in part, explains why so many children who have been sexually abused have difficulty sleeping. They try to stay awake, as if being awake will stop the sexual abuse from happening.

The child, as he or she becomes older, will appreciate the duplicitous nature of the sexual offender – often someone admired by others. Sexual offenders can speak eloquently against sexual offending and yet continue to sexually abuse. They can convey contradictory messages simultaneously. The consequence for the recipient of such contradictory messages is confusion.

Sexual abuse can be framed as loving. The child can be told they liked it or they wanted it, when their own experience is the contrary. A child can be made to give contradictory messages, such as saying they liked it when they did not. If their bodies responded to physical stimulation they can feel confused because one part of them may have said 'no' but another part of them said 'yes'. They will need help to sort out this confusion.

They may need you to be clear that you hear them and that you are trying to understand what they are going through. You may need to teach them to listen to you and to ask you questions if they don't understand. You may need to do the same to them. You need to give them feedback about what they are communicating to you.

When helping a child to recover from sexual abuse, adults can be confronted by contradictory messages which make it difficult to know how to respond to the child. The child can describe something that is very distressing and show no signs of distress. They may laugh when other people would cry. It is important to remember that the child, in order to survive the experience of sexual abuse, will have learned to smother their feelings. They may also need help to learn how to express their feelings, both verbally and non-verbally. Tell them you don't know how to respond to them when they give you contradictory messages.

If they have become very sexualised by the experience of sexual abuse, they can continue to use sexual gestures and postures to ask for comfort. They often do not realise there are other ways of doing this. They may also be unaware that most people would consider their manner sexually provocative. Until they are given feedback about how they currently behave, and alternative ways of behaving, they will continue to use the same behaviours and methods of communicating that they have always used. It is difficult for protecting adults to tackle this, but essential that they do so.

Developing appropriate personal authority issues

Sexual abuse is not only a sexual violation of the child, it is also an abuse of the authority adults have over children.

> He knew that he had power over me to do it. I couldn't do nothing back.
>
> (Alison)

The experience of sexual abuse impacts on the child's understanding and experience of authority. Unfortunately the abuse of authority is endemic in our society. Teaching children that it is wrong to bully or force someone to do something they do not want to do is fraught with problems because that is so often how people do things and get what they want. Experiencing sexual abuse can therefore reinforce a perception in the child that the world is composed of abusers and abused. It can lead them to avoid authority, to view it suspiciously, and expect it to be tyrannical. The responsible exercise of authority often cannot be recognised. So it is particularly important that the parental authority of the non-abusing parent be reinforced after the discovery of sexual abuse.[10]

It is also important that the child who has been victimised sexually feels comfortable with their own authority so that they can be responsible for their behaviour. They may need help to learn the difference between assertiveness and aggression. Having lived for years with a bully, it is unlikely that they will not have learned a lot about bullying.

Children who have been sexually abused are very perceptive

to power hierarchies. They understand and will challenge authority, or ally themselves to those they perceive as powerful. This can be functional as it is a useful skill to have in a society that is so preoccupied with authority. But it can also be dangerous. The abused child can be labelled manipulative, which carries very negative connotations. And there are clear gender differences with males being encouraged to assert their superior position in the power hierarchy, and females being punished for assertive or aggressive behaviour.

The issue of authority is relevant to all of us, but for those who have been sexually abused it is especially so. All too often children do not see authority being used effectively, even by those adults who seek to protect them. Also, the sexual offender will have undermined anyone else's authority, as a way of reducing its potential protectiveness.

Protecting adults are in the unenviable position of trying to establish the responsible exercise of authority while at the same time benefiting from the privileges bestowed on adults. But by struggling with these issues and discussing them with the children and young people you come into contact with, you will begin to challenge the authority of the abuser which for so long remained unchallenged in the child's life.

Dealing with the Consequences

This chapter has outlined some of the consequences of sexual abuse and drawn your attention to areas of concern for many children and young people who have been sexually abused. It is important not to underestimate the role your support and belief play in a child's recovery. It is also not the sole responsibility of the protecting parent to deal with all the consequences.

Recovery work is very demanding and often emotionally draining. The pain, distress, sadness and anger experienced by protectors can go on and on, and they are likely to feel lonely, isolated, frightened and overwhelmed by the task of helping their child recover.

I hope and pray we never go through anything like it again. We are still trying to get our lives back to normal . . . I don't think Alison and myself will ever get back to the way we were . . .

(Moira, Alison's mother)

You may need to remind yourself how things really were. Now that the sexual abuse has been discovered, the possibility of recovery or even discovery of parts of yourself, your relationship with your child, your friends and community is available to you.

Do not be afraid to ask for help and support for yourself and your child. You may think you are managing or you may feel utterly overwhelmed.

I know that as an ideal to be strong for your children is crucial and right and necessary; but from my experience of not just myself but of other mothers in my situation – we have been broken wrecks for all kinds of reasons . . . being strong has been something we tried to do and usually failed miserably, taking our children down with us.

Sometimes it is possible to feel that 'professionals' can expect the impossible because, in most cases, they do not know what it actually feels like and cannot comprehend the devastation . . . Most of us can be left feeling guilty that we are never strong enough, loving enough, though enough, un-neurotic enough, good enough . . .

(Tilla)

But remember – it would be unusual if you didn't feel like that. Protecting adults frequently have to take all of the responsibility and yet rarely have the authority to get what they need for themselves or their children. It is likely, in the circumstances, that you have done more than you think.

I used to think my mother was to blame. I don't now. At the group, we talked about it and I think she did enough for me. She believed me. All the other girls there, their mums didn't believe them and they were all in foster care.

(Alison)

Being at home with her mother who believes her makes it possible for Alison to manage her recovery work, take responsibility for herself and her future, and want more out of life than childhood memories of sexual abuse.

CHAPTER SIX

The Healing Process

This chapter is designed to help you identify situations when professional help might be warranted; to provide information so that the child receives the best possible help; and to suggest some of the issues you might want to take up with the child to begin the healing process.

But before any healing can begin, the child needs to be safe. First of all, you must have ensured that the sexual abuse has stopped and that the child is surrounded by a network of protecting adults.

It may be that you and other protecting adults can provide the best context for a child to recover. Children may prefer to talk to the people they are closest to, rather than a professional stranger. (This is generally true for younger children, whereas adolescents often prefer to talk to someone outside the family.) Certainly, the more knowledge and information protecting adults surrounding children have about sexual abuse, the issues which may arise, and how best to help a child recover, the more likely a child's speedy and full recovery.

Professional help, such as therapy, can certainly help sexually abused children and support the protecting adults, but it would be far more beneficial for the child if *all* the surrounding adults had access to the skills and expertise of professional child protection workers and could employ these to support children in their day-to-day living. Professional help should ideally back this up, not replace it. So, the following section of this book provides information about what is likely to arise once sexual abuse is disclosed, to give you the skills to best help your child recover.

The initial disclosure, of course, marks only the beginning of the healing process. There will probably be more to tell. The more the child is able to speak about their experience, the quicker they will be able to put it behind them. But in some cases, the child will not want to discuss the experience immediately. It can help to have a safe distance between an event such as sexual abuse and the talking part of the recovery process.

You may want to leave it to the child to indicate when they are ready to talk. But be careful that you are not encouraging the child to silence – or colluding with the natural tendency to want to forget the experience and not talk about it any more. You should signal to the child that you both know about the abuse and that you are available if they want to talk about it at some stage in the future.

In some cases the child may choose to start talking about the abuse at an inconvenient time; when there are lots of people around, for example, so that the conversation will not be private. If this happens, you should acknowledge that they have indicated a desire to talk about their experience, and then make a time when it would be better to continue the discussion.

Children may want to talk about the abuse at times when they remember or have flashbacks to the experience.

The memories I have always seemed so far away but now they keep getting closer and I remember things that happened many years ago. It's really scary. I can be doing something really normal and then suddenly I get the recalls of the past. Just little things but they really wind me up.

(Lisa)

This can be in situations that remind the child of the original sexual abuse, such as bedtimes or bathtimes. In these situations it is important that you reassure the child that they are now safe.

... Even now I think it still has an effect on me ... I was really scared and I didn't want to go to my maths lesson ... my teacher reminded me of my abusers – they were tall, he's tall and you have to look up like that . . . he's got a moustache . . . and, like, talks in a deepish voice. It scares me, but not enough for me to really show it.

(Natasha)

You may want to change routines around any trigger activities so they are less likely to remind the child or young person of their sexual abuse. It can be helpful to change bedrooms or rearrange the furniture in an effort to reduce unwanted memories. Living in the house where it happened will be difficult for the whole family, but particularly for the child who has experienced the sexual abuse.

Children often do not like to talk face-to-face about their experience of sexual abuse, preferring to talk whilst doing something else, such as washing the dishes or being driven in the car when the adult is in the front seat and they are in the back seat. The more distant approach seems to help the child discuss some of the more worrying aspects of their experience.

As the experience of phone lines has taught us, children will talk about their experiences of abuse on the telephone, which can be as anonymous as they wish, and gives them maximum control. They don't have to be looked at and so feel less exposed, and they don't have to deal so much with the reactions of the person listening.

For protecting adults supporting a child in the healing process, it is important to get the right balance between being interested and available, and being too intrusive and curious.

. . . [It's important] to let the person that it's happened to do some of the talking – like I noticed with my social worker when she was talking to me, she'd try and push words into my mouth, like, you know – and that's not what I wanted to say.

(Alison)

It is important to recognise that the recovery process is not accomplished overnight, but is ongoing. Every developmental phase may bring up new issues. Do not be surprised if the sexual abuse seems to become an issue at a later stage in the child's development. For example, many young women who were sexually abused become concerned about protection issues when they themselves become mothers. Adolescents can become confused, worried or distressed when they want to be physically intimate with peers but do not know how their earlier experience of sexual abuse will impact on this.

Remember that if such issues, concerns or problems do arise later, this does not mean that the work done earlier was not helpful. It merely indicates that more work should be done now, when new situations have triggered different concerns.

Occasionally, children will talk about the abuse too much. When they tell for the first time adults may – and should – stress that the child was right to tell, and encourage the child to feel good about having told. However the danger of talking too much is that the child might then start telling everyone, which can put them at risk. Other children may tease them about it; adults and children who are not aware of how to deal with sexual abuse may disapprove of and/or blame the child; and any adults who have a sexual interest in children may hear about it and recognise that this child will be an easy target. It is important that children are given identified trusted adults to whom they can talk. In the school situation, it can be helpful to have one identified teacher who is aware of the sexual abuse. In the extended family particular relatives can be identified as sources of support for the child.

It is important that all those who care for the child recognise the child's right to privacy and guard against the indiscriminate disclosing of information regarding sexual abuse. The appropriate involvement of the wider network surrounding the child needs careful consideration. And the child will need to know who knows about their experience and who they can talk to if they want to. If you are in any doubt about who to involve in the child's wider network seek advice.

Getting professional help

Recovery can take many forms, and if the child can put the experience to the back of their mind and get on with their childhood, this may be very functional. It does not mean they will never have to do some additional work on their experience of sexual abuse at a later stage, but additional work may not have to be provided by professionals. Often, life experiences in and of themselves can be healing. For example, a close friendship, a good relationship with a parent or parent figure, an understanding partner, can all contribute to a successful resolution of a sexually abusive experience.

> If it came back as a worry I'd share it with someone, 'cause here [at the foster family] I was always taught 'You share your worries', like a problem shared is a problem halved. I was always taught that ... like my nextdoor neighbour – she even wrote me a song on it ... Lean on me, when you're down and feeling blue, you know you can lean on me ...
>
> (Natasha)

In general, if a child is able to get on with developmentally appropriate tasks, there may not be a need for additional help, beyond information for parent and child, possibly some counselling, and access to resources.

But you should particularly look for professional help if, after the abuse:

(a) The child is finding it difficult to do things other children of the same age can do.

(b) The child is exhibiting problem behaviours which are beyond normal limits and have gone on a long time.

(c) Commonsense approaches have been unsuccessful in trying to reduce or eliminate problem behaviours.

(d) The child is old enough to participate in treatment and, where appropriate, wants help to sort out the problems.

But remember, professional help should ideally *back up* support that you, and other members of your child's network, will need to give your child, not *replace* it. You will need to have the skills to deal with, for example, difficult behaviours which may result from the child's acknowledgement of the abuse and the work the child does with professionals. If the child goes into therapy, for instance, they are likely to explore very traumatic issues which may trigger behavioural problems. If the adults surrounding the child on a day-to-day basis have no idea how to manage these behaviours then the child's recovery is likely to be hampered. The surrounding adults will need the skills to reassure the child that these behaviours – which, as we have seen, may previously have been functional to surviving the sexual abuse – are no longer necessary, and to teach the child to cope with their feelings in a different way.

If it is clear that a child or young person requires additional professional input, it is important that the primary caregiver feels confident in the skills, and is comfortable with the manner, of the professional who is undertaking the treatment work.

You can sometimes refer your family or child directly to a professional helper, especially if you are paying for your sessions. However, most often, referral for professional help is either through your GP, who should know what is available in your area, or through Social Services, who may be able to offer some help themselves. Most agencies involved in recovery work would want to know that the child protection issues had been dealt with as there is no point offering treatment to a child who is not safe.

Don't hesitate to ask questions about the service being offered. It may seem intimidating, but good professional workers should help to put you at your ease and explain clearly and simply what they do, why they do it, and how they think they can help.

The following is a series of issues you could discuss prior to the child or young person starting treatment. They should form part of establishing the therapeutic contract between the worker, the primary caregiver, and the child.

Expertise in and approach to sexual abuse work

Not all professionals will have had training in child sexual abuse as part of their qualification training. Do not assume that because someone has a professional qualification, they know about sexual abuse. Always check this, and if the professional does not have the relevant training and experience, seek other help. Additionally, the professional's views about sexual abuse might not correspond to your own. You may not feel comfortable with the way in which your child's experience is handled. If this is apparent at the outset it may be better to seek help from someone whose views more closely approximate your own. It is important that the professional helper is clear that sexual abuse is a real experience that is often traumatising and always disturbing for the child, and that it is the adult perpetrator who is responsible for the sexual abuse. If the professional helper is at all disbelieving of the child's experiences, it is doubtful that they will be able to help the child recover.

It may also be important to know to what extent sexual abuse will be the focus of the therapeutic work. Some professional helpers will work specifically on issues related to the sexual abuse, while others may employ a broader life perspective or be very non-directive in their work. If a child is too young to decide what will be helpful for them, it is important for the primary caregiver to help decide what suits an individual child's needs. Some children respond well to a very focused approach, while others benefit from a more non-directive style. The key issue must be what is best for the child at a particular stage, and to what extent the sexual abuse will be recognised as shaping the child's current behaviour or emotional distress.

Use your knowledge of the child to help you choose the professional help that fits with your child's temperament. A brief, focused groupwork experience is often extremely helpful, as many children gain a lot from being with other children who share the same experience of sexual abuse.

Liking and feeling comfortable with the person who is going

to work with your child is very important. Remember, you are entrusting your child's healing to this person, so you should have confidence in their ability to help sort things out, and they should be able to tell you how they think they can achieve this.

It is important that the child or young person knows that the professional helper is aware that sexual abuse has happened. Otherwise a lot of valuable therapeutic time can be wasted because the child keeps the sexual abuse secret as they've previously been told to do, and the professional helper is overly sensitive and does not raise the sexual abuse until the child does.

Confidentiality

Issues around confidentiality need to be clear at the outset. The difference between secrets, confidentiality and privacy needs to be spelt out for the child or young person and the primary caregiver. Because sexual abuse is often surrounded by secrecy, this aspect of starting therapy can be very confusing for everyone. Therapy should be a special time for the child. It is private and what is shared between the young person and their helper is confidential. However, if the child or young person wants to share the contents of their therapy sessions, they should be able to do so. It is important to ensure that therapy, while private, is not secret, as this is perhaps too similar to the secrecy promoted by the perpetrator when the child was being sexually abused. If the child is in a group context then they will have to recognise the need to respect other group members' privacy.

Sometimes confidentiality can be interpreted too rigidly, whereby primary caregivers are not given any information at all about the sessions. This is unhelpful because it appears to promote secrets between the child and one protecting adult which are not shared with another protecting adult. Clearly this will be more of a problem with younger children than with adolescents, who are more likely to understand the difference between secrets and privacy.

However, it needs to be made clear from the beginning what is private to the session and what will be shared with the adults who have a responsibility to protect the child or young person. Generally, anything that would indicate the child is going to harm themselves or cause harm to others should be shared outside the session. If the child makes new disclosures this should also be shared outside the session. This does not include amplifications regarding the original allegation, although technically this could constitute new disclosures.

Feedback

This issue is related to confidentiality. Primary caregivers should have some feedback regarding the sessions. With older children this can be done as a progress report which is discussed privately before being given to the primary caregiver and/or the professional who has referred the child for treatment. Children and young people can appreciate why adults need to have some idea about what is being discussed in their healing work.

It is also important to remember to give the child or young person feedback about their progress as well. Often the recovery process can seem very slow and changes hard to detect. Periodic reviews can be useful to remind everyone just how much has been covered already.

Availability between sessions

It is important to know how available the professional helper will be between sessions, especially if a crisis arises. This may be an issue for the primary caregiver and for the child, particularly for adolescents. Professional workers should be able to give clear messages about their availability. Professional helpers are not the same as friends and consequently are not as available as a friend or parent might be. This artificial construction of the helping session is part of what makes it useful and enables the abused child or young person to talk about painful experiences. The sessions are limited, usually to an hour in individual work sessions and longer for group or family work. The meetings take place in a neutral venue and not where the child was sexually abused. The child or young person is not expected to deal with the helper's feelings or problems, as they would be with friends.

The helper is there to listen carefully and give their full attention to what is being discussed. To do that, appointments are made at regular intervals. They can be from several times a week to once a month. Usually individual and group work is weekly. Family sessions may be spaced out to fortnightly or monthly. With weekly sessions, the child has to learn to manage their feelings as best they can in between sessions. Sometimes this is very hard, which is often why primary caregivers and the young person concerned want to know if they can telephone in between sessions if they get scared or upset. Sometimes it can be helpful for the child to write in between sessions because on the day of the appointment the child may not remember what it was that seemed so unmanageable before.

Timescale

It is helpful to both child and primary caregiver to have an idea how long the piece of work is likely to be. It may be that the child or young person is being considered for a groupwork programme that runs for a set number of sessions, or for a more open-ended contract of individual work. Either way there should be some idea about what level of commitment is being asked for from both the child who will be attending and the primary caregiver who may be accompanying. Sometimes open-ended work can seem too threatening. A limited number of sessions can feel too rushed. The younger a child, the more a focused and time-limited approach may be appropriate. As a primary caregiver you can help by discussing what you think would best suit your child.

Expectations

It is important for expectations to be clear at the outset. Clearly for younger children it is essential that they are accompanied to each session and picked up at the end, preferably by the same person. Adolescents may want to go on their own but they will need to demonstrate to the adults who care for them that they can do so responsibly. This means arriving on time and returning home safely. The primary caregiver, the helper and any other protecting adults need to check with one another that this is happening. Some young people may leave and return 'on time' but not actually go to their sessions.

Clearly there is also the expectation that the child or young person will attend the sessions offered regularly and will cancel appointments in advance if they are unable to attend. For anyone accompanying a child or young person to treatment work, the travelling to and from the sessions is often a time for additional discussion. This can be very positive and emphasises the important role that the accompanying person plays in the child's recovery process.

A professional helper should let you know that the situation will improve and give you an idea of the likely process. As mentioned earlier, it is extremely common for difficult behaviours to get worse once the child begins to discuss the sexual abuse, before they get better.

If there is a serious doubt about the likelihood of improvement, this should be discussed openly at the outset. This should be rare but it does occur, as in situations where a child requires very intensive work but resources are not available. In this case the work offered is not the best form of treatment, rather it is all that is available, and this may mean that the outcome will not be as good as was hoped for.

Some children and young people are so distressed that it is unclear at the outset which treatment will be useful for them. They may also be so out of control themselves that they will not be able to use treatment at this time. They may be acting out sexually by sexually abusing other children; or glue sniffing, drinking, or taking drugs; self-harming or overdosing. All of these very extreme behavioural disturbances need specialist resources to help. These children are much more likely to require residential placements rather than weekly one-to-one sessions, and may also need to be assessed by a child psychologist or psychiatrist.

If these children are living at home, the primary caregiver, as well as the young person, will need a lot of support. If the child is placed in a residential unit, the expectations the unit has of the primary caregiver should be made clear. Some units involve families and friends actively in their recovery programmes for residents. Some also like children and young people to return home at weekends.

All professional workers involved in caring for children and young people are expected to behave professionally towards them. It is gross professional misconduct for any professional to hit or in any way physically abuse; to have sexual relations or in any way sexually harass; to verbally abuse or humiliate any child or young person with whom they are working.

If your child tells you about any improper professional conduct, take it seriously and report it immediately to the statutory child protection workers. Professional workers are paid to be protectors of children, and a breach of duty in this respect is totally unacceptable. Guidelines have been produced by various professional groups to monitor and maintain good practice.[1]

Criteria for termination

It is important to know if there are criteria for termination of the treatment work. It may be that the child or young person must attend a certain proportion of the sessions offered. They may also need to demonstrate an ability to use the sessions. If they spend every session in silence or refuse to participate it is unlikely to be a beneficial experience in the long run. It is often difficult for children to refuse treatment when adults who care for them are extremely keen they should have it. Often the only way to express their dissatisfaction is to refuse to participate in the session itself.

On a more positive note, how will everyone know that the time has come to finish the work, especially if it is an open-ended contract? What are the signs or indicators that the child or young person has recovered enough to no longer need professional input? It can be helpful to discuss this directly with the child or young person. Who decides when the work should finish, or if it should start again?

I know I would need help again if I started isolating myself again – or if I started to think about it all of the time. I don't now so maybe it's over.

(Alison)

. . . I needed help again. I was always crying and everything and that was the first time I ran away. My social worker's boss thought I should go to – one of them men you can go to and talk to . . . I don't get all the different names, like psychologists and psychiatrists . . . but I don't really want to go and see a man, I'd rather see the woman I saw before.

(Natasha)

If a child has had a good relationship with a previous therapist, and they feel they need additional help, it is best to see if that person is still available to offer help. The shared knowledge and experience often mean they can get down to sorting out the current difficulty more quickly.

If the previous therapist is not available, the child or young person may have clear ideas about who or what kind of therapy they would find useful. Natasha was clear she wanted to see a woman. A clear preference should be respected.

Termination of a particular piece of work does not necessarily mean that all therapy has to stop. If one type of treatment such as group work doesn't appear to be helping another type such as one-to-one can be tried; if the child or the therapist cannot continue because someone is moving new therapists can be found.

Abrupt endings should be avoided. Both the primary caregiver and the child should know when the work is scheduled to finish. The ending should be positive, leaving the child/young person feeling they can manage or that arrangements have been made to find someone else to carry on.

Evaluation of change

It is useful at the outset of treatment work to think about the signs that will indicate that your child is beginning to recover from their experience of sexual abuse. You may want to discuss this with the professional helper. If a primary caregiver is specifically looking for symptom reduction, then clearly they will think treatment work will finish when the distressing behaviours have gone. Not all professional helpers would see the reduction of symptoms as an indication that treatment work can finish. So it is important for everyone to be clear why the work is being undertaken, what will be discussed, and when the work will end. Professional helpers should be able to explain simply why they work the way they do, and what benefits the child will gain.

Other treatment issues

It is important that primary caregivers are involved at the outset of therapeutic work, if only to meet the professional worker. But clearly, if an adolescent makes the referral themselves, this would not be appropriate. Children and young people may also use phone lines to help them recover. Even if the primary caregiver comes to know about this, it would not be appropriate for them to interfere.

Consideration needs to be given to the gender and race of the professional helper. Many children, especially adolescents, are very sensitive about gender and express a clear preference for working with women (particularly, of course, if they have been sexually abused by men). For children from minority ethnic families a professional helper from the same cultural group is preferable. If this is not possible it is important that the professional helper have a clear understanding of the limits of their cultural knowledge. Where the child and the professional helper are from the same community, it is important that issues regarding confidentiality are clearly spelt out.

Where it has not been possible to provide children or young people with a professional helper who meets all of their requirements regarding race and gender, it is important to discuss this at the beginning of the work and recognise that there may be aspects of the experience that will be especially difficult or even impossible to share.

Treatment work should not cause further harm to the child or young person. Consequently attention needs to be paid to the timing of the offer of treatment as well as to the fit between professional helper and client. It may be helpful for a child to have a break between different pieces of treatment work so that they can consolidate gains. For example, they may have just finished a group or some family work when they are referred for individual work. An uninterrupted stream of treatment work can be counter-therapeutic in that it becomes the habitual way of dealing with problems. It can also undermine the natural healing network that surrounds every child by not actively incorporating the child's surrounding network into the recovery process.

If, as a primary caregiver, you feel that the treatment is doing more harm than good, it is very important that you discuss this with the professional helper as soon as possible.

If a child or young person clearly does not want to continue with their treatment work, it would be wrong to force them. With younger children, the primary caregiver can discuss the issue with the professional helper. With adolescents it can be hard to find the balance between speaking for them and letting them find their own voice.

In an earlier example, Natasha expressed a clear preference for working with a woman after being referred to a man.

Q: Were you able to say that?
Natasha: No, I didn't say nothing 'cause, like, she [the team leader] was doing most of the talking –
Q: Did you think about asking to see the woman you saw before?
Natasha: No, I was thinking about it but I was scared to say anything –

In this situation she needed someone to be her advocate. She recognised she needed more help and had a clear idea who might be able to help. The professional workers heard part of her message – 'I need help' – but then moved too quickly into providing a helper without considering that Natasha might have some ideas about what kind of help she wanted based on her previous experiences of therapy.

Goals of treatment work

Treatment work should help the child or young person and their primary caregiver achieve a sense of mastery over an experience which violated them and took away their sense of control.

> I think [therapy] really helped me, like, come to terms with the fact that I was abused – that other people do it but you can get over it in the end.
>
> It helped me share my feelings, like – half the time I didn't have to say 'cause, like, [my helper] knew. It was as though she was a mindreader and really knew what would help me . . . She thought of the best way possible of bringing that out – of helping . . . she used pictures, she wrote that song . . . I still got bits of that song everywhere . . . She helped me come to terms with the fact that it wasn't my fault; that it happens to other people; that you can be helped, that you can get over it and you can start afresh and, like, you don't always have to be living in the past – living with that cloud over your head saying 'It can happen again'.

(Natasha)

Treatment work should convey a strong sense of being believed to the child or young person. It should affirm their feelings, whatever they may be, and help them explore feelings that are less comfortable and maybe even scary. It should increase the individual's self-esteem. To help the recovery process it is important that the issue of responsibility for the sexual abuse is explored, starting from the premise that adults have a responsibility to protect and NOT abuse. It is important that the child's sense of blame is addressed, that regardless of the fact that the strategies they used for protecting themselves are often interpreted as contributing to the abuse, they are not to blame for what happened.

It is important to recognise and name the survival tactics they employed. It can help a young person immensely to view something like bed-wetting as a survival tactic. It may now be a habit, but it may once have been the most effective way of terminating an episode of sexual abuse.

Helping the child, young person or the primary caregiver identify triggers for challenging or out-of-control behaviour is essential. Giving the child a sense of mastery or control means they must be able to recognise when they might lose control, and learn other ways of coping with the feelings that are triggered.

> Blanking out just happens and I don't always know why it has happened. [In one way] it is good because it helps me to say what I want without getting any emotion, or memory of saying it. Now that it has been pointed out to me that I do it I can see that I used to do it before, especially when I was with him.
>
> (Lisa)

There are many different ways for this to be achieved – either in work with a professional or with the primary caregiver.

Different types of work to help children heal
Treatment work can be offered on a one-to-one basis, in groups, and with other family members. Sometimes a combination of all three is useful. All of the issues laid out earlier in this chapter regarding the setting up of clear ways of working in advance are relevant, regardless of what type of treatment is offered.

Family work
Working together as a family unit can be helpful. Sexual abuse is something that distorts family life by promoting an atmosphere of secrecy and dishonesty. If, during and after the

investigation, a family member is excluded from the family home, this will have profound effects on all family members. It is important that the family can discuss this with an outsider, who should be more able to raise some of the difficult issues.

Offering help to all family members may make it easier for the child who was targeted to use their treatment time. For example, in a follow-up of young women who attended a group-work programme, the issue of additional help for other family members was raised.[2] The young women made a number of points and comments about their experience and views:

- I felt guilty that only I got offered groups.
- My brother is very blocked about it. He felt he let me down. He's been different to me ever since. He's never hugged me or comforted me. He was so important to me. I looked up to him.
- I think groups for mums would have made me feel better, knowing she was getting help too.

Of the fourteen young women interviewed, five said it would have been helpful if their mothers had been offered help; four specifically mentioned their brothers; and one specifically mentioned how unhelpful she had found family work because the perpetrator was also present.[3]

If a family is referred for treatment, this should not include the perpetrator unless he has had considerable treatment himself, and the child whom he targeted is ready for this to happen.[4]

Group work

Having the opportunity to discuss issues in groups with others who have shared a similar experience is a good way of practising the far harder task of talking with one's own family. All of the young women followed up for the evaluation mentioned above thought the groups were useful. They all thought it was most valuable because it broke down the isolation they felt.[5]

Instead of, like, you just being by yourself, it's like you have

> to come up with all the answers – everyone puts in answers
> and everyone works together . . .
>
> (Natasha)

> . . . the group gives you a chance to talk about your feelings
> with someone else that's been through it . . . we'd all have
> to listen to each other.
>
> (Alison)

A group-work experience should help individuals feel connected to others who have shared a similar experience. It can be
helpful to make sure this will happen by checking out some
basic information about important issues such as the racial
mix of the group.

In the girls' group follow-up, one young white woman
remarked, 'There was only one coloured girl and she didn't
come very often.' It may have been that being the only black
girl in a group of white girls did not help the young woman
feel less alone but rather emphasised her isolation from her
community.

> The group itself was mixed racially. The group leaders were
> two women – one was Indian and one was black. The group
> really helped. We talked about it – they knew a lot . . . the
> women who ran the group – they were really good. Before
> the group I sort of felt I was the only one.
>
> (Alison)

If your child has a disability, hopefully at least one other group
member will too. A very different experience from the rest of
the group or something that sets one member apart will need to
be handled very carefully in a group setting. If your child is
different from others in the group in any way, it may be advis-
able for you to decide to ask for one-to-one work instead.

It can be helpful to find out if there are any local groups.
These groups may be run by professional helpers or function
as self-help groups. But remember that some of the issues

raised in looking for help for your child are just as important when using a self-help network.[6]

If the group-work programme has an outline of the topics covered, it can be useful for primary caregivers to have these. They can then follow up or watch for particular signs of distress after certain sessions. Many group-work programmes often run parallel caregiver groups.

Individual work

Most of this chapter has been addressing issues in relation to one-to-one work. This is perhaps what is most likely to be offered if you seek professional help. One-to-one work can range from counselling and play therapy sessions to individual psychotherapy. There is a wide variety of approaches, so it is helpful to ask questions about the work as outlined in the previous section.

If you don't like what your child has been offered, you can refuse treatment. Clearly the central role of the therapist in one-to-one work emphasises the need for you to trust this person to help your child. In group or family work there are other people who also play a crucial role in the healing process and the importance of the individual therapist is less crucial.

Sometimes a child or young person cannot work with the professional who has been assigned to help. It can be difficult to raise this but it may be crucial for you and the child, as well as being important feedback for the professional. The issues of gender and race are again more potent in one-to-one work. If you or the child have any doubts or reservations about the work these should be raised at an initial meeting. It may be helpful to start with a limited number of sessions and review how these have gone before committing yourself and the child to a protracted piece of therapeutic work.

Some of the issues that may come up in both individual and group settings relate to the child's feelings towards the perpetrator, their non-abusing parent, and their siblings. Often they feel unable initially to discuss these in a family context. Having their own space to air these feelings is very important.

Managing challenging behaviours

Many children who have been sexually abused have very challenging behaviour even after the sexual abuse itself has stopped. In part this may be because they still feel unsafe. It is also likely that they will be having unwanted memories or flashbacks to the experience of sexual abuse which will trigger the challenging behaviour.

> When I listen to certain music it reminds me of him and what he did to me. I feel really high and out of it. It is almost as if I'm in a world of my own – sort of blanked out – which is what I did when he abused me. I'm not in control of my actions, I feel really weird, as if anything could happen and it wouldn't affect me. And I don't care who sees me or what they think of me or what I'm doing. At these times I'm most likely to cut up or drink myself silly.
>
> (Lisa)

It can be helpful to remind yourself that some of these behaviours helped the child or young person to cope with the experience of sexual abuse. In Lisa's case, the blanking out helped her endure what her abuser did to her. Now when she blanks out, she hurts herself.

Until you can teach or help the child to find other ways of dealing with their distress, they are likely to carry on with the challenging and often disturbing behaviour. You may see a clear pattern to the behaviour. There may be specific triggers – similarities that remind the child of their experience of sexual abuse. For example, whenever Natasha saw her mother on contact visits, her eczema always got worse.

To help you identify possible triggers to unwanted memories, think of dates; time of day; all of the five senses – seeing, hearing, smelling, touching, tasting; certain situations; certain types of people; certain feelings.

> Sometimes, when I get angry or upset, you know – it comes back . . . or when you read these sorts of things in the paper.
>
> (Alison)

In one-to-one work, Lisa made the following list of things that still brought back memories for her:

> Cortinas
> Capital Radio/Radio 1
> Pink jumper
> Metal case full of bits
> Dole forms (UB40)
> Blue eyes, blond hair, tall, skinny, beer gut
> Jeans, blue jumper
> Ribena cartons
> Tissues
> A long list of dates and specific places

It can be helpful to think of things to do that reduce the negative consequences of the triggers. In many cases primary caregivers and the child or young person themselves do not recognise the triggers, and the behaviours that follow are often very negative and destructive.

> I like to cut myself because I get so frustrated that I don't know what to do with the anger and upset inside me – Also to make myself look uglier so that it will never happen again.
>
> (Lisa)

Helping Lisa identify what made her angry was part of disrupting the pattern of her self-harming.

Sometimes there is a context in which problem behaviours are appropriate. But with self-harming, there is no acceptable context. Not only was Lisa helped with identifying triggers but also to find something else to do when she felt frustrated, angry and upset. She was also reassured that her appearance was not what caused the sexual abuse.

Ten-year-old David used to get very upset and then urinate in his bedroom. His mother was able to connect the urination on the carpet with his fear and upset following his experience of sexual abuse by his stepfather. She talked to him about his feelings and put a bucket in his room. She told him if he was worried and upset but unable to come out of his room at night he could urinate in the bucket. Every day she would clean the bucket. If he had used it the night before she made a safe time for him to talk about what had scared or upset him. Gradually he used the bucket less and less, and talked with his mother more and more.

His mother made it possible for him to express his feelings in a safer and literally more contained fashion. She recognised that he was still not able to put some of his feelings about his experience of sexual abuse into words. She provided him with an alternative and followed up with safe time to talk about his worries. She understood that using the bucket at night was a signal to her that he had something to say but needed her help to say it.

Sometimes primary caregivers will need to discuss ways of managing challenging behaviour with a professional helper. Together they may identify the triggers for it and provide alternatives for the child or young person that make them feel more in charge or in control of themselves and their feelings.

If, as a protecting parent, there are now episodes of behaviour you see in a different light, it is important that you share this with your child. It is important for them to know that you did notice certain behaviours but that you incorrectly assumed they meant something else. For example, Asha, whose stepfather sexually abused her, found that if she slept in her sister's bed with her sister he would leave her alone. Her mother noticed Asha's requests to sleep with her sister and thought it odd because they seemed to fight so much when they were together. After a while she would encourage Asha to be grown up and sleep in her own bed. It never occurred to her that Asha slept in her sister's bed to escape being sexually abused.

Treatment work with protecting primary caregivers and children should go a long way towards resolving the emotional consequences of sexual abuse identified in Chapter 5. However there are times when specific, additional pieces of work may need to be done, such as preparing children for legal proceedings, or helping children move on to alternative families or residential units. These may be time-limited pieces of work with a clear focus and end-point in mind.

The healing process begins with the disclosure or discovery that sexual abuse is happening. The consequences of the experience often lead to periods of time when the child is distressed and unable to get on with age-appropriate tasks. In these cases it may be necessary to seek professional help. This doesn't mean you have failed your child because you can't make things better. It underlines your commitment to sort out the difficulties and use whatever help you can to do it.

Specialist resources are scarce and this chapter tries to help protecting adults become more aware consumers of those resources so that their children can get the best from them. It also emphasises the need for professionals to work closely with primary caregivers, to make best use of each other to maximise the potential for healing. Useful resources and addresses are included in the appendix.

Healing and recovery work can happen in different ways and places, not just with a professional therapist. Remember you are teaching your child to learn to take care of themselves, to be able to get help when they need it and to use it effectively.

Sexual abuse need not dominate someone's life for ever, especially if it has been stopped. The healing process should aim to put the experience of sexual abuse into a wider context and life experience – one which allows the individual to develop their potential and to express themselves without fear of disbelief but with the courage it takes to survive.

CHAPTER SEVEN

Using the Statutory Agencies

There will be situations where involving professional child protection workers will be necessary. Understanding how the statutory child protection agencies are organised and how they work will help you get the best from them when you need them, and so this chapter describes the agencies and the various possible consequences of using them.

Reporting abuse

Statutory child protection agencies are agencies which have a legal duty to investigate allegations or suspicions of child maltreatment. Once a suspicion has been referred to them it has to go through the legal system. (The only other agencies obliged to take legal steps are the police and the National Society for the Prevention of Cruelty to Children – the NSPCC.)

If you have reported sexual abuse or suspected abuse to a professional such as a doctor or a teacher, they are *strongly advised* to report it, but they are not obliged to do so. If you want them to activate a formal investigation you should make it clear that you want them to report the sexual abuse or suspected abuse to the child protection agencies. If you are unsure, but the professional you confide in thinks the concerns should be reported, you should be told that this will happen. Professionals should only refrain from letting you know if they feel the risk to the child to be extremely high, and that your role as protector is unclear. In such cases, they may pass on concerns without informing you.

This chapter outlines the criminal and civil proceedings that may arise as a consequence of sexual abuse. These include investigations, medical examinations and case conferences which are common to both court processes. Criminal Injuries Compensation is also discussed.

Remember, if you do decide to go to a child protection agency you are likely to need other support as well. The issues involved in statutory intervention are often complicated and confusing, especially when you are feeling low and confused yourself.

There can be very little response initially, followed by a lot of involvement with professionals and then nothing at all.

> Quite a lot of people came down but then they just sort of vanished at the time you need them most.
>
> (Alison)

It is important that protecting parents have support networks they can rely on to help them throughout the recovery process and not just through formal investigations.

The Child Protection Committee
Child protection services are overseen by Area Child Protection Committees (ACPCs). These Committees are made up of senior officers from all the agencies involved in child protection work. This includes, principally, Social Services, Police, Education and Health. These Committees draw up the policies and procedures that operate at a local level.

ACPCs meet at regular intervals throughout the year to review child protection services. They are required to publish an annual report of their work. They often oversee training in child protection and try to review cases where children have not been protected.

Case conferences and the Child Protection Register
Concerns regarding sexual abuse can come from a variety of sources. Most frequently they come from adults who have a primary responsibility in caring for children. This includes primarily mothers but also other family members and relatives, as well as health visitors, nursery workers and teachers.

If a specific allegation of sexual abuse is made to a statutory agency there is a duty to investigate that allegation. However, if concerns are raised that abuse *could* be happening, with no specific allegation that it *is* happening, the professionals may choose to monitor the situation for a period of time rather than immediately instigating a formal investigation.

The first stage in the monitoring process is usually to call a case conference. A case conference is called by the local authority (that is, your local council) and attended by workers who have knowledge of the child who is the focus of concern. It always involves a representative from the police and Social Services, and usually health and education staff are represented by the relevant professionals (for example, the child's GP, health visitor, teacher or head teacher).

Many ACPCs encourage parental participation at this level, so if you are invited to attend it would be very wise to go.

Of course many parents find case conferences daunting and intimidating, and you can seek support through agencies such as the **Family Rights Group** or other parent support groups. It can be useful to attend with someone else who can help you go through any information or plans that are produced. And it is helpful if you can prepare for the case conference by writing down your concerns and any questions you may have.

The purpose of a case conference is to consider whether a child is at risk and what further steps need to be taken to protect the child from future risk or to reduce the current level of risk. A worker should be identified who will oversee the implementation of any protection plan.

A case conference can decide that a child's name be placed on the Child Protection Register, which is a register kept by the local authority of all children who are currently believed by the state agencies to be at risk of 'significant harm'. It can also recommend whether further investigations should take place and whether or not child care legislation is needed to protect the child. Case conferences should also identify resources to help non-abusing parents reduce the risk of further sexual abuse.

The common focus of all the people who meet at a case conference is the protection of the child. If there is a conflict of interests between the parents and the child, the child's interests come first.

Case conferences are then usually called again at regular intervals to assess whether the level of risk has been reduced, remained the same or increased, and whether or not the child's name should remain on the Register. Case conferences will stop when the level of risk has been reduced and there is no need for further professional monitoring or for intervention from child protection agencies.

Child protection case conferences can vary tremendously, even within the same local authority. What happens in a case conference is very dependent on the skills of the chairperson and the input of all participants. If you attend a case conference and are not happy with what happened, you can complain. All councils must have a complaints procedure which should be publicised. This should tell you how to go about making a complaint in your area. Call your local authority for details of the procedure if you need to.

If you are not happy with the way the local authority has dealt with your complaint, you can contact your local councillor, the **Ombudsman**, or your MP.

As a parent at a case conference you have some clearly defined rights. These have been summarised by Ann Lewis writing about parental participation in child protection work:

- The right to know the name of the worker responsible for your case and how to contact them.
- The right to know what the workers will do and what legal powers they have in relation to the child protection issues identified.
- The right to be listened to.
- The right to give explicit consent to or refuse intervention such as a medical examination or interview (except where this conflicts with the rights of your child,

or there is a court order saying the intervention should
take place).
- The right to be provided with information relevant to
  making choices about whether a medical examination
  or an interview, for example, should take place.
- The right to share in exploring problems, goals, tasks
  and criteria for a successful outcome.
- The right to know what is said or written about you
  (except where this conflicts with the rights of others).
- The right to have access to records and to the deliber-
  ations of professional helpers.[1]

You could use the above as a checklist when you go to a case
conference so that you make sure that you get all you can out
of the occasion.

Investigative interview

In situations where a specific allegation of sexual abuse has
been made, or the index of suspicion is extremely high,[2] it is
most likely that the child will be interviewed by both a police
officer and a social worker. (This is referred to as the Police
and Social Services joint investigative team.) The interview is
likely to be video-recorded. The purpose of the video-recording is to save the child having to repeat themselves over and
over again. It is now also possible for the video-recorded
interview to be submitted as evidence-in-chief if the case goes
to a criminal trial.[3] This means that the child does not have
to tell what happened to them in court as their recorded
statement can be shown. But the child will still have to appear
in court to be cross-examined about their statement.

The purpose of the investigative interview is to assess
whether or not a crime has been committed, and if child
protection measures need to be taken because there is evidence
that the child is at risk. The child's parent must consent to
the interview being conducted. If consent is withheld and child
protection workers are very concerned about the level of risk
to the child, they may seek an Assessment Order,[4] which, if

granted, allows them to interview the child without the consent of the parent.

Once the interviews have been completed a case conference is usually called. This should be within eight days (and definitely no later than fifteen days) of the matter coming to the attention of the statutory agencies.

Very little information is given to non-abusing parents about how to prepare a child for giving a statement to the investigators. But you should try to explain to your child the purpose of the interview, since children who understand the purpose will give clearer statements.

In general, it is better if your child does not give their statement with you present. Children and young people can be very protective towards non-abusing adults and find it difficult to talk with them there.

Sometimes, as in Natasha's case, the sexual offender may be present which makes it almost impossible to talk.

> I think the worst bit that I didn't like was my mum and my dad in the same room – it was like, 'Oh, no . . .' At one or two points . . . my dad was in the same room when they were talking and the dolls were in the bag on the side [and I thought] they'll say something . . . I was scared of that.
>
> (Natasha)

> I felt really dirty. I felt embarrassed saying what had happened. [The police] were okay. They were really nice – [they explained things to me] and that's when it hit me. I thought, 'Oh, God, what have I done?' They took a statement off of me. And then it was just all solicitors and social workers . . .
>
> (Alison)

Many who work in the field of sexual abuse fear that involving both parents, one of whom may be the perpetrator, will increase the risk to the child by alerting the suspected perpetrator to professional concern. This is coupled with a worry that non-abusing partners will not engage with the protection plan and will support the suspected perpetrator at the expense of the child's current and future protection. It is important that you show that you can put your child's safety first and make it possible for other people to help assess the risk, even if this means facing that your partner has sexually abused your child.

It can be extremely helpful for a parent to directly tell the child to talk to the investigators, by saying, for example, 'I want to know what, if anything, has happened to you, and if you are not able to tell me I want you to tell these people.' This gives the child permission to talk and often frees them from worry or fear.

Medical examinations

In many cases a medical examination will also take place. Again, this cannot be done without parental consent. However if there is a high level of concern, professional child protection workers can use an Assessment Order to allow a medical examination to be undertaken without permission.[5] On the whole parents rarely refuse permission for a medical.

These examinations should be done only by trained paediatric forensic practitioners. These are doctors who specialise in working with children and have been trained in the gathering of medical evidence for legal proceedings. This should reduce the possibility of multiple medical investigations being conducted.

A medical examination may provide corroborating evidence of sexual abuse. If the case goes on to court the medical examiner will be required to give evidence regarding their findings. (Remember, though, that medical evidence is found in only a minority of cases of sexual abuse. Lack of medical evidence DOES NOT mean that sexual abuse has not taken place.)

Who should accompany the child or young person to the medical needs consideration. Ideally it should be someone with whom the child feels safe. But sometimes young people prefer to be examined without someone they know being present.

Medical examinations often evoke very powerful reactions

from the child or young person. So it is very important that they understand why it is happening and are given feedback after.

> I went downstairs into this other place ... they wanted to check me to make sure nothing was wrong ... I remember this man and rubber gloves and I was just thinking, 'Oh, my God, what is he going to do?' And, like, he checked out my privates and I was just thinking, 'Oh no no no, I want to get out, I want to get out'. My foster mum was there at the time – and he made me go to the toilet, and I couldn't go ... so the nurse put water on to try and help me go ... I went in the end and that was the last I heard about it. But I had to do this more than once. [I think] if children *have* to be [examined], then just once, not more than once. If it happened to a boy I think it should be a man doing it. But if it happened to a girl ... it should be a woman – 'cause you won't really want a man to do it.
>
> He explained that he wanted to make sure everything was alright ... well, I thought there was something wrong and that I had to have this [examination] done to make sure I was alright.
>
> (Natasha)

So, before the medical examination, make clear to the child that the purpose of the exam is to check for signs of sexual abuse, and to ensure there is nothing wrong with them physically. Check with the professionals organising the medical that the gender of the doctor is not the same as that of the perpetrator. It is also important to explain to the child that there may well not be any visible signs of abuse and that this in no way suggests that anyone thinks that the child has lied.

Q: Do you know why they give children a medical when there has been an allegation of sexual abuse?
Natasha: To see what they've done and like, to make sure it's true and ... they're not lying.

Q: How do you think they could tell from a child's body whether what the child said is true or not?

Natasha: There might be marks.

Q: And if there were no marks?

Natasha: It *might* mean they're lying [but] sometimes people are careful enough not to leave marks.

The results of the medical examination should always be discussed with the primary caregiver and, where appropriate, the young person. This is an opportunity for you as the primary caregiver to ask any questions regarding the child's physical wellbeing. The issue of sexually transmitted diseases should be raised, especially in the light of HIV infection. Tests may have to be repeated at a later stage to check for this. It may be better for these to be done through special clinics where confidentiality is guaranteed, especially in cases of HIV infection where there are considerable long-term consequences if a test is done (i.e. the child may be refused life insurance, mortgages and health care insurance in the future).[6]

There may also be other medical complications that are not evident at the initial examination. These can include bladder and bowel problems and/or reproductive difficulties due to undetected/untreated sexually transmitted diseases, or where cervical competence has been compromised. Where young children are concerned, a primary caregiver must be given this information. With adolescents it can be more helpful for them to be alert to some of the potential medical consequences and encouraged to seek sympathetic medical treatment in the future if they have any concerns.

Legal proceedings

After gathering the evidence from the investigative interview, medical examination and Social Services assessment of risk, a case conference will then consider what else needs to be done to protect the child. Civil or criminal proceedings or both can then be initiated. Criminal proceedings focus on the apprehension and conviction of the alleged perpetrator of the crime. Civil proceedings deal with the welfare of the child.

Criminal proceedings

All the evidence amassed by the investigators is passed on to the Crown Prosecution Service (CPS), and they decide whether to start criminal proceedings. If there is sufficient evidence, a possibility that a conviction can be gained and it is considered in the public interest, a criminal case may begin.

Sufficient evidence would include a clear verbal statement by the child when they were being interviewed by the Police and Social Services joint investigative team indicating that a crime has been committed, and who the perpetrator is. It is now possible, due to a change in the law, to convict on the uncorroborated testimony of a child.[7] Previously the child's statement needed to be supported (corroborated) by medical evidence and/or a witness.

You should be told if a criminal prosecution will *not* be mounted, preferably with some indication of the reasons. Often very young children (under five) are thought to be too young to be cross-examined in court and if a child or young person is not able to be cross-examined on their statement then it is unlikely the CPS would recommend going to trial.

If the case does go to trial, there can be a considerable time delay between the reporting and the trial itself. Furthermore, only in exceptional circumstances would the alleged perpetrator be kept in police custody. This means that the child and the protecting adult will have to deal with the perpetrator being out in the community and possibly putting pressure on the child to retract the allegation.

In some cases, the perpetrator admits to the offence. This means that the child will not have to go to court. The case will be dealt with more quickly and it is more likely that a lenient sentence will be passed.

It is important to know exactly what the perpetrator has been charged with if you are going to support your child through criminal proceedings. Sexual offences have very specific definitions within the law.[8] For example, incest relates to sexual intercourse only between a man and a woman he knows to be his granddaughter, daughter, sister or mother (or between a woman and a man she knows to be similarly related). Sexual intercourse by a stepfather with his stepdaughter if she is under sixteen (the age of consent) is not considered incest but unlawful sexual intercourse (USI). The criminal charge of rape could also be used but the child or young woman would have to show that the sexual intercourse took place without her consent. As this can be hard to prove legally, the charge of USI is used more frequently. Sexual contact between family members of the same sex or sexual acts other than intercourse fall outside the incest law and would result in other criminal charges being made, such as indecent assault or buggery.

Each of the different charges carries a different maximum penalty. This varies depending on the charge and sometimes the age of the victim. Rape, buggery or USI with a girl under thirteen years of age and incest with a girl under thirteen carry a maximum penalty of life imprisonment.

You may get very little notice that the case has come to trial. You may initially be given a rough idea when it might happen and then suddenly be notified a few days before the case goes to trial.

The child's evidence is usually heard at the beginning of the case. If a video-recording has been made this will be shown in court as the 'evidence-in-chief'. Children and young people under seventeen can be linked to the court by video. This means they do not have to sit in the courtroom itself but in another room on their own with a court usher and perhaps one supporter. A TV screen in the court relays the picture and answers given. They will be questioned and cross-examined about the allegations.

A child's testimony will be scrutinised and defending barristers will ask questions which try to raise a shadow of doubt. They can try to cast doubt on the child's credibility or confuse them by asking very convoluted and complicated questions.

As unjust as this may seem, it is their job. A criminal prosecution must prove beyond a shadow of doubt that a crime has been committed by the alleged perpetrator.

It is important to remember that children can feel empowered by giving evidence. If you are supporting a child through court proceedings there are books that have been written both for supporters and children to help with this process. These are included in the appendix. And there is clear evidence that preparing children for criminal proceedings is helpful and reduces the stress of the experience.[9] Most preparation work concentrates on giving children information about the court procedures. It can also be helpful to visit the court prior to the actual appearance.

Not all Crown Courts are equipped with live video links so it is important to check what is available in your area. Remember the time lag between the investigation and a case coming to trial in Crown Court when preparing children, as preparation work is clearly best done a little in advance of the actual appearance, not months before. And too much preparation can make the child more rather than less anxious.

It is also important for adults supporting children through court proceedings to avoid any suggestion that they may have coached the child. This means suggesting questions the child may be asked or answers to possible questions. It is best to encourage the child to tell the truth, to do their best, and not to worry if they get confused or do not understand something.

It is important to understand that the child is a witness and as such is helping the judge and jury decide what has happened. This is an important opportunity to reinforce some of the issues that have been raised about who is responsible for what. In criminal proceedings the child is providing information. The jury is responsible for the decision about whether or not the case has been proven beyond a shadow of doubt. The judge decides what the sentence will be.

It can be unhelpful if supporters of the child become obsessed with obtaining a guilty verdict. This can put extra pressure on the child. Should the defendant be found not guilty, it can also make them feel responsible for the verdict and naturally think they did not do a good enough job giving their evidence.

Being clear with children about who is responsible for the trial outcome can also be reassuring if an offender is found guilty and sentenced. In this case the child can be reassured that the judge has passed sentence and that the responsibility for punishing the perpetrator is not on their shoulders.

It may be that you will also have to give evidence because you witnessed an episode of sexual abuse or the child told you first about the allegation. Some preparation for appearing in court will be helpful for you as well. Go with your child to the court. Find out where you can get tea or coffee and other practical arrangements like transport and toilets. You should be given a copy of your statement to go through prior to giving your evidence, and it will be useful to have read it and thought about it before your appearance.

You will have to appear in court and face the accused. This can be distressing and difficult. You will be examined and cross-examined on your evidence. If you get confused or in a muddle you can say so and correct any misunderstandings that may have arisen. Give your answers to the judge. By speaking out, you are supporting your child. If your child knows you believe them, the outcome of the court case will matter less.

Remember that it is possible that you and your child could go through the whole criminal court case and the perpetrator could be found not guilty.

At the trial, when they found out about what happened – Mum wouldn't let me go – they came back and told me. I just couldn't believe it. My social worker was just sitting there and she didn't know what to say really, and my mum – she was angry . . . I just couldn't believe it . . . He got away with it. The policewoman who took my statement – when I gave her a day, she looked back on the calendar and got the wrong date so we lost the case ... just because of one date I lose the whole thing, just like that.

(Alison)

Alternatively, the sentence may be much more lenient than you, your support network and your child believe is fair.

Maybe he has spent time stuck in a cell but that will never make up for what was done to me ... the judge who put him away didn't put him away for long enough as far as I'm concerned. I just got so much anger inside me for him. It's almost like he committed the crime but I have to suffer for it ... I'm scared that he will come after me and start threatening me.

(Lisa)

You should be prepared to comfort the child and to stress that the outcome is not the child's responsibility but that of the legal system.

Press coverage
Sexual abuse cases often get reported in local papers. The identity of the child or young person should not be revealed, but this can often be deduced by people in the community. Only rarely will sexual abuse cases attract national media attention. This usually happens when there is a legal precedent being set (as in the case of DNA fingerprinting in a sexual abuse case, or a private prosecution being mounted), or where the sexual abuse is considered unusual (as in the Epping Forest satanic abuse case). But any press coverage can be disturbing.

If you feel your child has received unfair treatment in the press you can complain to the **Press Council**. Keep a copy of the article concerned, as it can be used as evidence of the distress caused to the child if you apply for Criminal Injuries Compensation.

Civil proceedings

It is extremely difficult to prove beyond a shadow of a doubt both that sexual abuse has taken place *and* the identity of the person who has sexually abused the child. For this reason, most cases of sexual abuse are heard in civil proceedings. Only a very small number of sexual abuse cases go on to criminal proceedings, the highest proportion being in cases where the perpetrator has admitted the offences.

In civil proceedings the welfare of the child is paramount. The standard of proof is lower in that findings of sexual abuse can be made on balance of probability, whereas in criminal court such a finding has to be proved beyond a shadow of doubt. For this reason it is possible for a finding of sexual abuse to be made in a civil court which is not matched by a conviction in a criminal court.

Civil proceedings cannot convict an alleged perpetrator but they can ensure protection for the child. If the evidence suggests, on balance of probability, that the child has been sexually abused, and, if possible, that on balance of probability the perpetrator can be identified, then the civil court will rule on such matters as whether the child should be removed from the family home; whether the perpetrator must stay away from the child or whether continued supervised contact is in the child's best interest. But before going to court everyone concerned will encourage co-operation between statutory agencies and parents. It is much preferred that agreement can be reached without going to court. If a parent is clearly protecting their child from further sexual abuse and actively engaged in helping the child recover from their experience, the necessity for civil proceedings is minimal. Court cases arise when local authorities disagree with parents over the best course of action, where children need to be removed from their families of origin, or in matrimonial proceedings where issues of custody and access might hinge on an allegation of sexual abuse.

Every attempt is made to keep children either in their families of origin or in their extended family network. If there is no agreement between the statutory agencies and parents on this, it is possible the child could be removed either on an Emergency Protection Order or an Interim Care Order. Also, a parent can ask that the child be 'accommodated' by the local authority for a period of time.[10] A child is also likely to be removed from the family if a non-abusing parent does not believe the child has been sexually abused and yet the balance of evidence suggests that they probably have.

If the case does go to court, the video-recorded interview, medical examination information and Social Services assessment of risk will all form part of the evidence in civil proceedings.

In civil proceedings the child will have independent legal representation. The court appoints a guardian ad litem (GAL) to represent the child's best interests and views. This person will meet with the child and all significant adults including child protection workers. The GAL will then make recommendations to the court regarding the child's future. The child also has access to a solicitor who usually acts in tandem with the GAL unless there is disagreement between what is in the best interests of the child and the child's expressed view.

In this case, the solicitor will put forward the child's view (for example, I want to go home and live with my mum and dad) and the GAL will put forward what they consider is in the best interests of the child. In situations such as this, it is also possible that another independent solicitor will be appointed for the child and the previous solicitor and GAL will continue together.

Civil courts are slightly less formal than Crown Courts. There is likely to be a minimum of three solicitors – one for the parents, one for the child, and one for the local authority. If the parents disagree with each other they will each be represented by different solicitors. It is also possible for grandparents and other members of the extended family to be represented if they want to be directly involved in the child's future.

As the child does not have to appear in civil proceedings, the adults can try and sort things out together. If they fail to reach agreement the judge will listen to everyone's case and make a decision. It is essential that a protecting parent get good legal advice from a solicitor who is a member of the Child Care Panel.

In civil cases, although children need not appear it is important for them to know what is going on.

> I went to see the judge and I saw the court that it happened in . . . she tried her best to explain to me that they ask, like, my mum questions . . . they were making decisions that I shouldn't live with my mum, and that I'll get access once a week and that was changed to every two weeks, and then monthly.
>
> And then 'cause it kept getting me upset my social worker went to the judge and got it stopped.
>
> (Natasha)

Criminal and civil proceedings can both happen at the same time. Usually civil proceedings go at a faster pace, often because there are no identified protectors within the child's network, which means that a safe place must quickly be found for the child.

In Natasha's case there were civil proceedings to remove her from her family of origin and place her with foster parents. Her contact was suspended with her mother through civil proceedings, in part because her mother continued to deny that Natasha had been sexually abused, which was unhelpful to Natasha's healing process. There were no criminal proceedings.

In Alison's case there was a criminal case that resulted in an acquittal. There were no civil proceedings because Alison's mother believed her daughter, no longer lived with the perpetrator, and did whatever she could to help Alison recover.

In Lisa's case there was a criminal prosecution which resulted in a conviction. Lisa's mother requested that Lisa be 'accommodated' under The Children Act because she could not deal with Lisa's distressed behaviour. This request was dealt with through civil proceedings.

When the accusation of abuse is raised as part of matrimonial proceedings, matters can become very complicated. This is because matrimonial proceedings specifically deal with issues of custody and access. If the court decides to rule that the father must have access to the child while the proceedings go through the court, or the final ruling of the court is that the father must be allowed ongoing access, then it is possible that you may find yourself being ordered to allow contact between your child and someone you consider to be harmful to them. Clearly this is more likely to occur if the court considers the allegations of sexual abuse to be unfounded.

It can be helpful to use the statutory agencies in contested contact and custody cases where sexual abuse is an issue. In these cases it is important that the child is interviewed and that all of the evidence is considered. If you think your child has been sexually abused on an access visit, it is essential that this is investigated, preferably by child protection agencies. If there has been no previous sign of emotional distress in your child and they suddenly become distressed, and then tell you that they have been sexually abused, access should be suspended pending a full investigation by the child protection agencies.

The issue of continued contact is difficult to assess. In part, you and the court will have to consider if the child is old enough to protect themselves, and if contact is in the child's best interest. If the situation is unclear, it may be appropriate for contact to be supervised by a protecting adult who feels empowered to intervene if there is any inappropriate interaction.

If, as a protecting parent, you are confronted with an enforceable contact arrangement, the importance of teaching your child how to protect themselves is heightened. You should also tell them that sending them to see the perpetrator of the abuse is not your choice.

It is important to explain to your child that it isn't your decision to send them on access visits (even if supervised). Try to explain and comfort them when they are upset about going. Reassure them it isn't your decision.

(Kiera)

It may also be helpful to record your child's behaviour before and after contact, including what your child says to you and significant others.

Kiera meticulously recorded her daughter's behaviour following the supervised weekly contact until the matter was resolved in court. The court ordered an assessment to take place and access was suspended until the assessment was complete. Her daughter's symptomatic behaviour – including fearfulness, bed-wetting, and compulsive masturbation – reduced dramatically over the time of the suspended access. As part of the assessment Jasmine was ordered to see her father. Following this visit, Jasmine's symptomatic behaviour returned. She began to wet the bed and masturbate and it took two weeks for these behaviours to subside. The meticulous record-keeping was vital in establishing the link between Jasmine's symptomatic behaviour and contact with her father. On the basis of this, as well as the other evidence presented, it was possible to recommend a cessation of access until such time as Jasmine could protect herself and express her own view. At the time the ruling was made, Jasmine was only four.

No criminal proceedings were brought, but a finding of sexual abuse on balance of probability was made in civil matrimonial proceedings. Jasmine had not made a clear verbal disclosure to any of the formal assessors in her case, but she had repeatedly and consistently told her mother, her aunt and her maternal grandmother about how her daddy hurt her. Here is an example from her mother's diary:

13 May 1991
J. asked to see Daddy. T. said do you want to? J. replied no – don't like him. T. asked why, what does Daddy do? J.

said he hurts me, he hits me on my back and on my tummy and pats my boo boos. During the conversation she kept trying to touch her boobs and look down her top. Got in a temper a few times, keeps hitting herself and saying she doesn't like and love herself.

14 May 1991

While getting J. into her nightie she said he's not hurting me. T. said who? J. said Daddy. T. said why? J. said Daddy hurts me in this nightie. T. asked what does Daddy do. J. said he pulls it and touches my bottom. T. asked what J. did. J. said I said no and Daddy cried.

7 August 1991

Didn't wet bed. When getting ready in bathroom asked if her daddy would hurt her when she saw him. I said no. She said I ask him not to.

7 November 1991

Wet bed. Not too bad. Still hitting herself on the head. Had a dream during the night. Woke up crying. Asked her what the dream was about. J. said frightened Daddy at my window. Came in my bedroom. Restless all night just wanted me to cuddle her.

These recordings give a clear picture of the child's distress, and were a vital part of preventing any further sexual abuse.

Taking legal action in sexual abuse cases can be extremely complicated. It is often very difficult to predict what might happen in any one case and legal results may not be ideal or what you expected. It is therefore essential to ensure that you and your child have information, advice and support at every stage of the process, not just from the statutory agencies but also from your own network as well.

In Jasmine's case, her mother was able to make good use of her extended family network as additional protectors for her child as well as enlisting the support of statutory agencies.

Her daughter's recovery was assured by her protective action. A protective network surrounding the child and the primary caregiver, plus the professional child protection workers, should work effectively together to protect the child or young person.

Criminal Injuries Compensation

Anyone who is a victim of a crime of violence and has reported the crime to the police is eligible for Criminal Injuries Compensation. If statutory child care agencies are involved, or the child has been interviewed by a joint police/social work investigative team, the child should be able to apply for criminal injuries compensation. It is not necessary for the case to go to a criminal court, or for there to be a guilty verdict if it does. A finding of sexual abuse will be made on the basis of statements taken and evidence collected by the investigators. Balance of probability will be used – the same level of proof as is used in civil proceedings.

It is a paperwork exercise and the forms can be filled in on behalf of the child. There is a three-year limit on applications, but this can be waived until the child is twenty-one years old as long as there is a written record of the sexual abuse. The application will be assessed and a decision made usually within nine to twelve months. If you wish to appeal the decision, there is a time limit of three months within which you can do so.

In 1991–92 there were applications from 2,881 children who had been sexually abused,[11] 1,661 of them by a member of their family.

Awards vary, depending on the seriousness of the injury sustained as a consequence of the crime. Under new proposals a system of fixed payments is to be introduced, ranging from £1,000 to £17,500 for sexual abuse deemed most serious (repeated rape and buggery for more than three years).

In sexual abuse cases the 'damage' may not be immediately evident. The bulk of the harm will be classed as psychological suffering. Infrequently there will be actual physical injuries.

However, the longer-term consequences, both in terms of psychological functioning and reproductive health, are difficult to predict. Whether or not there is any evidence of 'damage' at the time of reporting, compensation should always be applied for. It is the child's right to be compensated as a victim of a crime of violence.

Payment can be withheld or reduced by the Board for a number of reasons. These include a delay in reporting to the police, not co-operating with the authorities, and perhaps most controversially, certain conduct or lifestyles which are seen by the Board to have contributed to the occurrence of the offence (frequently referred to as 'contributory negligence'). This is especially relevant in sexual offences, where the guidance notes specifically mention any 'provocation or otherwise on the part of the victim'. This discriminates unfairly against female children who are much more likely to be seen as contributing to their assaults by virtue of gender alone. It is rare to hear of young boys being viewed as provocative or 'asking for it'.

Payment can also be withheld if the offender is likely to benefit from an award being made. This is relevant for children who apply for compensation where rehabilitation of the offender to the family home is being considered. If a young person has convictions for criminal offences, they are not eligible for compensation.

The scheme is also clear that no payment will be made for any child born as a result of the sexual offence. However it should be possible to include in the claim the psychological effects of termination of pregnancy, possible compromise to future reproductive health, and the impact of such an early pregnancy on future pregnancies, especially given the context of conception.

Any award made to a child will be placed in trust until they reach the age of eighteen. It is possible to access some monies from time to time to purchase certain items, however on the whole the bulk of the award is usually left in trust. To access it, you would need to write on behalf of the child (or the young person could write directly), outlining what you want the money for. It is possible that the request would be turned down. Often the procedure for withdrawing money early is so cumbersome that parents end up leaving the money alone.

If the child or young person receives other monies, such as social security, payments made under insurance or civil actions, or pensions, the compensation may be reduced or the benefit withheld until the amount falls below the allowed savings threshold. For this reason many young people are advised to use up the money quickly on something substantial. This may be a trip, or items for their home. It can be helpful if a protecting parent encourages the young person to spend the money on something connected to their recovery. Without (and sometimes with) adult guidance, many young people fritter away the award money. This can be in part because it is seen as 'dirty money', but it can also be a big responsibility which, at eighteen, is too difficult to manage.

The process for applying for compensation is as follows:

1. Apply in writing on either an application form available from the police or by writing directly to the **Criminal Injuries Compensation Board.**
2. Police report is submitted.
3. One Board panel member makes a decision.
4. Acceptance of offer or appeal within three months of offer being made.
5. If an appeal is made this is heard in front of a three-member panel. This panel will not include the individual who made the original offer. The panel is likely to be made up of predominantly white, middle-class male lawyers. Usually the parent or guardian of the child is required to attend. Many people go to solicitors for advice and are represented by them at the appeal, but this is not essential.
6. All evidence is gathered. This includes written reports and oral evidence given, which may include expert opinion. All witnesses will be cross-examined. However

this is not as formal as criminal, or even civil, proceedings.

7. A decision will be made which is then not subject to further appeal. This decision could be less than the original award, but this is quite rare. Usually a higher award is made.

All the information used to decide on the award will be made available to the applicant. This includes police statements. This can be helpful as you will be able to see what the original decision was based on.

Ann, a young woman who was received into care at fifteen following disclosure that she had been sexually abused by her stepfather, applied for compensation. She received a letter from the Board indicating that the Board did not consider her to be a victim of a crime of violence. This official reply was devastating to her and she was encouraged to appeal. An appeal would mean disclosure of the material on which the one panel member had based his opinion.

Ann decided not to appeal as she did not feel she had the emotional energy to carry on fighting to be recognised as a victim of a crime of violence. It was likely in her case that the police reports suggested she was not telling the truth. However at an appeal it would have been possible to produce additional evidence to support her disclosure, such as the social work report and expert opinion from her psychologist.

So, compensation awards are not always straightforward. You might, for example, have to deal with an outright rejection as described above. You should also carefully consider how the child will understand the award. In one family where both children, a brother and sister, were made substantial awards, the understanding of the children was markedly different. The boy, who was older, understood that the award was a form of compensation for the pain and suffering he had experienced as a consequence of the sexual abuse. The girl thought she was being paid for what had happened. Given that money was an integral part of her experience of sexual abuse, it was important for her mother to help her understand that the compensation award was not another form of payment for sex.

To use statutory agencies effectively, a protecting parent will need to deal with a lot of information and often conflicting advice. There will be times when the whole process will feel out of control and you may wish you had never got involved in the first place. Do not stop thinking about protecting your child. They may need to be protected from some of the possible negative consequences of statutory interventions. Let your child guide your decisions. Not all children can manage the pressure of a criminal case in Crown Court, but many do. With reassurance and support it can be a very powerful experience that helps the child's recovery. Some children may require extra coaxing to have a medical or to be interviewed. It is best to take one step at a time and give yourself plenty of time to think.

The services provided by statutory child protection agencies are primarily offered to non-abusing parents. However other primary caregivers, such as residential social workers and foster parents, as well as members of the extended family, may need to support a child or young person through a range of statutory interventions. When a child or young person has become disconnected from their family of origin, the need for other protecting adults to support them is even greater.

> I was feeling really ill on the way [to court]. I didn't understand half the things going on. My residential social worker had to go into the witness box. She was really nervous but was great. She made me feel secure while I was feeling insecure. I just felt so close to her in the courtroom. I was holding her hand all the time.
>
> (Lisa)

For all protecting adults using the statutory child protection services, interviews and medical examinations and case conferences will need to be considered, followed by a case conference. After that, you should be able to identify professionals who will be able to help you through any further statutory work. If you get confused take notes, keep a record of your questions, and ask for written summaries of the issues raised in your meetings with professionals.

Don't hesitate to bring someone else with you to consult and discuss any issues raised in these meetings that may need an immediate decision. If you need time to think, ask for a short break, so you can talk in private.

Statutory agencies and court proceedings, both criminal and civil, should empower protecting adults by increasing the range of protective options available to them. Taking legal action is also the clearest possible signal you can give to a sexual offender that you will not be silenced and overpowered any more.

AFTERWORD

For the children and protectors in this book, the responses to their disclosures of sexual abuse have been varied and often contradictory. Most of the children and young people are on the road to recovery because they have been believed and supported by enough protecting adults.

For Natasha there was no criminal prosecution, but on balance of probability in civil proceedings her sexual abuse by her father and stepfather was acknowledged. Her mother was unable to accept this. As a consequence Natasha has lived away from home in a foster family with her brother, David. She remains on a Care Order and has no contact with her family of origin.

David was accommodated because his parents were unable to manage his care. He had severe epilepsy which has caused physical and intellectual handicap. He has very limited language. Like Natasha he was sexually abused by his father and stepfather. However, he was also sexually abused by his mother, which Natasha witnessed. It was hard for Natasha to define this as sexual abuse for a number of reasons: it was what she had grown up with; David was unable to name his experience himself and Natasha was reluctant to do it for him; and sexual abuse by women is often harder to name for reasons relating to social expectations of women and their behaviour in relation to children. There were no criminal proceedings in connection with David's sexual abuse. The civil proceedings removing him from his family's care did not deal with allegations of sexual abuse because Natasha had not yet disclosed. She remained living at home until David's foster mother, whom she saw regularly when visiting her brother, became concerned that Natasha may have been sexually abused. This activated the statutory child protection investigation that secured Natasha's safety and confirmed what the foster mother had thought had happened to David.

For Alison there was a failed criminal prosecution. Her perpetrator denied sexually abusing her despite Alison's mother witnessing him doing so on one occasion. When she found her partner sexually abusing her daughter, Alison's mother contacted the police. Alison's mother believed everything her daughter told her. She terminated her relationship with her partner and Alison has remained at home with her mother and sister.

Lisa's perpetrator admitted sexually abusing her but minimised both what he did and how long he had been doing it. He told the court he loved her and the local press reporting the case seemed sympathetic:

This is not a case of an evil man – it is a case of a sexually naïve and immature man who *allowed his heart to rule his mind*.

He was not motivated by evil or sexual gratification – he became emotionally and sexually attracted to her and *developed a boy/girl relationship*, albeit there was a great disparity in their ages [24 years].

A psychiatrist said [he] was *genuinely bewildered and remorseful* . . .

The material highlighted in italics in these quotes are explanations which were provided in court by professionals involved in defending Lisa's perpetrator and which were reported in the press. These professionals did not help Lisa's perpetrator to come to terms with what he had done, and to get the help he would need if he were to stop sexually offending against children. The perpetrator's minimisations and distortions were acceptable to and supported by the wider professional system. In this case, the perpetrator admitted what he had done, which meant that Lisa did not have to prove that what she said was true. His admission almost certainly resulted in a more lenient sentence. He received two concurrent sentences for sixteen months. He was not required to seek treatment.

Lisa's mother could not deal with what had happened to her daughter. Lisa lived separately from her family of origin, in residential care, for many years after her disclosure. She now lives independently. After a long period of no contact, she sees her mother and siblings regularly.

Jasmine's father denied sexually abusing his daughter despite her clear verbal accounts and medical evidence indicating that she had been interfered with. In matrimonial proceedings, a finding of sexual abuse was made on balance of probability. Jasmine's mother is seeking a divorce. Jasmine lived with her mother and sister throughout the investigation and civil court proceedings. Jasmine's father had a range of alternative explanations for the evidence, including: a plot by his in-laws to get rid of him; someone else had sexually abused his daughter and she had mistakenly named him; any hypothetical inappropriate touching by him of his daughter's genitals was only accidental.

There was no criminal prosecution despite strong medical evidence of sexual abuse. Jasmine was too young to give evidence in criminal proceedings and did not make a clear verbal disclosure in the formal investigation interview. Jasmine was considered safe in her mother's care. Additional help was offered to facilitate the recovery process. Jasmine's father's request for contact was denied in matrimonial civil proceedings until Jasmine was old enough to protect herself from him.

Asha's stepfather was convicted and sentenced to seven years' imprisonment for sexually abusing Asha. Her mother and extended family all believed her. She remained living at home with her mother and siblings. There were no civil proceedings because Asha's mother protected her. Asha's mother is seeking a divorce.

Evelyn, despite disclosing very clearly at two and a half that her daddy 'fucked her bum', remained living at home with him and her mother. Her parents explained away her disclosure by saying she was hyperactive, she said 'fuck' when she meant 'smack', and that the constant urinary tract infections from which she suffered were normal. They had professional witnesses who supported them and no further legal action was taken by the local authority. Officially, **Evelyn** was not sexually abused. There was no criminal prosecution because **Evelyn** did not repeat in the formal investigation what she had said to the nursery officer. Even if she had done she would have been too young to proceed with a criminal prosecution if the alleged perpetrator had denied committing the offence, which he did. The local authority failed to secure protective measures through civil proceedings.

Ann, who was denied Criminal Injuries Compensation because she was deemed not to have been a victim of a crime of violence, remained in the care system. She was not believed by anyone in her family of origin, although the local authority thought, on balance of probability, that she had been sexually abused by her stepfather. She now lives with her two children and battles with her depression which gets on top of her from time to time. She has no contact with her family of origin who have excluded and ostracised her for speaking out. There was no criminal prosecution because the police did not believe **Ann**. Her mother agreed for her to be accommodated and then initiated no further contact with her daughter.

Bonnie's father did not pursue his request for continued access to his daughter. No legal ruling was made in relation to **Bonnie's** allegation against him. **Bonnie's** mother and stepfather and the mother's side of the extended family all believed **Bonnie**. There was no criminal prosecution because **Bonnie** was considered too young to give evidence. There were no civil proceedings regarding child protection because the local authority felt **Bonnie** was protected by her family.

Heston and **Norleen** remained living with their mother, who was ordered by the court to allow their father to continue to see the children despite her concern that he had sexually abused both of them. The court ruled that there was no evidence, on balance of probability, that sexual abuse had occurred, and thought that the allegation arose out of an acrimonious divorce dispute. **Heston** and **Norleen's** mother faced imprisonment if she did not comply with the court order to allow her ex-partner access to their children.

Keith was in residential care when he disclosed sexual abuse by a male residential worker. There was no criminal prosecution because of the time lapse between when the abuse happened and Keith's disclosure. However there was an internal inquiry which, on balance of probability, believed what Keith had disclosed, and the worker was dismissed.

Vanessa lived with her mother who initially believed her baby was being sexually abused by her male partner. There was no criminal prosecution, nor was there any involvement with statutory child protection agencies. The matter was heard in matrimonial proceedings because Vanessa's mother did not want her partner to have any contact with the child. There was no finding of sexual abuse made during the proceedings and contact was granted to her partner. Shortly after she became reconciled with him.

Karen disclosed that her stepfather had been sexually abusing her after she had run away from home and was living in a residential unit. Her mother did not believe her. There was no criminal prosecution. Despite Karen's concerns for her younger brothers and sisters who remained living at home with her mother and the stepfather who had sexually abused her, the local authority did not remove them. Karen was told by her mother that she could not speak to her siblings about her experience of sexual abuse and if she did, she would not be able to see them any more. Karen kept in contact with her siblings who eventually came to her for help because the same thing was happening to them. Karen was able to protect them as she was living independently.

Kelly was removed from her family of origin and placed with foster parents. All her siblings were also removed and placed in separate foster placements. She disclosed experiences of sexual abuse from a number of adults, both male and female, in her extended family, including her father. There has been no criminal prosecution. In civil proceedings no finding was made regarding the allegations of sexual abuse because the general level of care in the family home was so poor that Kelly and her siblings could be removed on the grounds of neglect. Kelly has no contact with her father or other members of the extended family. She has limited and supervised contact with her siblings and her mother.

Many of the above results of the disclosures of sexual abuse are very poor in terms of criminal convictions. However, in a significant number there is a protecting adult who believes the child and is able to help the child begin the recovery process. Where there has been a failure to protect, one can only hope the child finds the resources to recover and the courage to tell again should the abuse continue. Sexual abuse is unlikely to stop spontaneously, so for Evelyn and Vanessa, who needed protecting adults to intervene on their behalf, it is likely that the sexual abuse will continue.

There have been campaigns for legal reform. The introduction of video-recorded evidence in criminal proceedings is one result of successful campaigning for changes in the law on sexual offences against children.

But it can seem that with every step forward there are other impediments. The legal protection offered by criminal proceedings is not uniformly distributed to the whole of the community. The most vulnerable sections of the community – the very young, the physically and intellectually disabled, those who do not have language or who do not have English as a first language, those who have a psychiatric history – are *less* likely to have their cases put forward into the criminal arena and conversely *more* likely to be convicted if they are the *subject* of an allegation. In part the cases are less likely to be put forward in these situations because these children are less likely, or indeed not able, to make clear unequivocal verbal disclosures of sexual abuse.

I could tell – get things sorted and I can share my problems . . . but David can't – like it's all locked up in him and he can't let it out. I think that's why he gets hyper and hysterical sometimes. I feel sorry for him – because I could tell . . . but he still can't *tell* anyone.

(Natasha)

The factors listed above are thought to affect the credibility of the witness. Anything which can be construed as making an individual, for whatever justified or unjustified reason, less credible, makes it more difficult for a criminal prosecution to be mounted.

The converse – that vulnerable members of the community are more likely to be convicted when they are the subject of an allegation – is related to the difficulty they may have in mounting a defence against the allegation and also other people's misperceptions about who sexually offends.

In the examples given above, there is a clear indication that the ethnicity and class of the perpetrator have an impact on the punishment the perpetrator receives: **Natasha**'s perpetrator was white – her mother disbelieved her and she was sent away; **Lisa**'s perpetrator was white – he received strong support from professionals and the media, as well as a lenient sentence. His position within the community was never jeopardised. On his return from prison, he continued to attend church. Lisa, on the other hand, became disconnected from her family and no longer attends the church to which they both belonged.

Ann's perpetrator was white – she was not believed by the police or her family and was excluded and ostracised for speaking out; **Bonnie**'s perpetrator was white – there were no civil or criminal proceedings; **Karen**'s perpetrator was white – there was no criminal prosecution and no support from the family – Kerry had to remove and support herself; **Kelly**'s perpetrator was white – there were no criminal proceedings and no findings of sexual abuse made at civil proceedings; **Heston** and **Norleen**'s perpetrator was white, they and their mother black African. A court order ruled that their mother faced imprisonment if she denied the perpetrator access to her children. One black British perpetrator was sent to prison for seven years and the only perpetrator denied access by the courts to his daughter was not white or English, but Mediterranean.

It is important, therefore, that we understand that the way we currently deal with child sexual abuse reflects all the prejudices and inequalities that exist in our society. Child sexual abuse does not happen in a vacuum. It comes out of the society in which we live. If we are to reduce the risk of sexual abuse and more successfully overcome its effects, we must also tackle the broader inequalities that exist. We need to challenge the abuse of authority that underpins exploitation of vulnerable groups in our society. Potential protectors need to widen the issue of child protection to include not only sexual abuse but all other forms of abuse, including the emotional and sometimes physical violence that accompanies racial and sexual harassment.

An experience of sexual abuse is an extension of the pervasive sexually aggressive culture by which we are surrounded. It can either confirm for the child that the world is indeed made up of the abused and the abusing, or it can challenge the child to find the alternatives.

We should encourage children to participate in protecting each other as well as themselves, to foster a sense of joining together to avoid being solely dependent on the powerful adult who can protect, but who can also abuse.

> Paula, my friend, came to protect me ... she would press the horn if he tried anything.
>
> (Lisa)

As protectors, we also need to help children learn not to bully and abuse others, particularly when children have been taught to target vulnerable members of the community in order to attack and exploit them. We need to try and stop other adults teaching children to adopt such inequalities and prejudices. Children learn about institutionalised hatred from the adults around them and adults should take responsibility for monitoring and challenging other adults when we see such views being fostered.

Child sexual abuse is complex, and ways of bringing it to light and dealing with it are often complicated and unpredictable. Very clear information about sexual abuse, how to recognise it, how to reduce the risk of it happening to children, and how to minimise its effects, should be given to children, parents and every adult who comes into contact with children in their day-to-day lives.

We need to have sensitive monitoring that can identify children who may be more vulnerable to sexual abuse because of previous experiences of sexual abuse, their position within the wider community, or the behaviour of their parents. We need services that will help those children who have been sexually abused to tell and get the help they need to recover. Protecting adults form an essential part of all these strategies. Professional child protection agencies will only ever deal with a minority of cases – usually those where the situation is extremely serious and community interventions have failed to help.

The active participation of the wider community in the task of protecting children is therefore vital. For children from the dominant group there will be a greater number of positive images for them to aspire to, whereas children from minority ethnic groups have to cope with unhelpful racist stereotyping. An experience of sexual abuse can make a child want to reject fundamental aspects of themselves which can include gender and racial identity. It can, as we have seen, also jeopardise the child's membership in the wider community. Strong protective adults from the child's own community are important role models for the child and the key to a positive and successful resolution of an experience of sexual abuse that does not jeopardise the child's future within their community.

Sexually abusive behaviour is unacceptable and we all need to do everything we can to make sure it is not allowed to flourish. Only organised networks of protecting adults will effectively outmanoeuvre sexual offenders. A haphazard individualistic response is unlikely to stop or reduce the risk of sexual abuse in the long term for the majority of children.

This book has aimed to provide the knowledge and information needed to inform children and protecting adults of the risks of sexual abuse; to teach the responsible exercise of authority; to learn to express anger and outrage safely and constructively; and to develop safer communities for children and their protectors.

Getting support for yourself and your child may often be the first step towards establishing a network and experiencing a sense of community. Being in contact with children puts adults in touch not only with a child's perspective but also with other adults who care for children. They, in turn, may be more receptive to concerns regarding the safety of children than you think.

Recent tragedies regarding children, such as the death of Jamie Bulger, abducted while shopping with his mother and then murdered by his juvenile abductors, serve to highlight the need for confident intervention in challenging inappropriate behaviour in public. Those same skills may be needed in your own life. Working towards a safer future for any one child should mean a safer future for all children. The monitoring and supervision you provide for your child or for children you come in contact with should extend to other children and in turn influence the adults they come in contact with. Sharing the responsibility to protect ultimately strengthens the protective network.

Understanding the reality of the experience of sexual abuse will help you to discover your own capacity to protect. Through protecting, you will come to know your own authority; find the strength to bear witness and the courage to speak out on behalf of others; and learn that the voice of a protector is a voice that will not be silenced.

APPENDIX

Resources and Useful Addresses

The following resources section is divided to correspond with relevant resources related to the topics discussed in each chapter. Within each category, resources are arranged alphabetically by resource title.

The lists are not comprehensive but provide a good range of materials. Before using any material with a child, be sure to go through it yourself first. You need to know what is in the material so that you can answer any questions a child might ask. This is just as relevant for older children and teenagers as it is for young children. The former are more likely to read the material and not ask any questions of you.

Resources can also date quickly and do not always reflect key aspects such as race, gender or disability in the stories or examples used.

You can ask if your local library or school has this material. If they do not, encourage them to stock child protection material, check that it is still there and update it regularly. Many children use books to find answers to problems that they feel unable to discuss with adults. ISBN numbers have been provided (where they are known) so that finding and ordering books is easier.

A list of useful addresses is also provided.

Videotapes
These are distributed by a number of companies but the following two have a wide range of videos on the topic for different audiences:
Albany Video Distribution, Battersea Studios, Television Centre, Thackeray Road, London SW8 3TW (Tel. 0171–498 6811; Fax 0171–498 1494);
Educational Media Video & Film Ltd, 235 Imperial Drive,

Rayners Lane, Harrow, Middlesex HA2 7HE (Tel. 0181–868 1908/1915; Fax 0181–868 1991).

Many resources can be obtained through your local Health Promotion Units. They can advise or assist you in obtaining material. Videotapes and training materials can be viewed but not borrowed at the Health Education Authority, Hamilton House, Mabledon Place, London WC1A 9TX, during working hours, Monday to Friday. Booking is essential (Tel. 0171–383 3833).

Bookshops will order books for you, especially if you can provide all the details given here. However there are some specialist outlets that have consistently offered an excellent range of material on child protection issues, such as **Bookstall Services**, 86 Abbey Street, Derby DE3 3SQ (Tel. 01332–368 039; Fax 01332–368 079) which offers mail order services; and, **Learning Development Aids**, Duke Street, Wisbech, Cambridgeshire PE13 2AE (Tel. 01945–63441; Fax 01945–587 361) offers an extensive range of health education material for children and those with learning difficulties. Primarily designed for use by professionals but easily adaptable.

Section 1: Reducing Risk
The resources listed in this section cover a range of issues from protecting children from sexual abuse to how to encourage them to be aware of their bodies and to deal with all sorts of unacceptable behaviours, such as bullying.

CHAPTER ONE
Resources
Videotapes

Breaking Silence, Tollini/Future Educational Films (1985) (58mins.)
Distributor: Albany Video
An American collection of personal testimonies from survivors

of sexual abuse, mothers of sexually abused children and perpetrators. There is a mix of both male and female, black and white participants. Designed for use with adults or older teenagers as an introduction to the issues involved in sexual abuse.

Changing Time, L. Summers (1977) (20mins.)
Distributor: Cine Nova: 113 Roman Road, London E2 0HU (Tel. 0181–981 6828)
An autobiographical film which re-examines the director's childhood experience of sexual abuse from her position as an adult. It interweaves old family photos and film footage with present-day commentary and images. Suitable for adults and older adolescents.

Crime of Violence, A. Droisen (1986) (52mins.)
Distributor: Glenbuck Films, c/o BFI, 21 Stephen Street, London W1P 1PL (Tel. 0171–957 8938)
A documentary with both theoretical discussions regarding sexual abuse and personal testimonies from adult survivors of childhood sexual abuse. There is one male survivor. The women who participated come from different backgrounds and include both black and white women. A useful overview of issues for adults and adolescents.

Secrets Sounds Screaming, A. Chenzira (1986) (25mins.)
Distributor: Cine Nova
This American video recounts the story of a mother discovering her daughter has been sexually abused by her partner. Additional comments provided by other survivors highlight the issues of disclosure for the child and her mother. Aimed at adults and older adolescents.

Through the Maze of Child Abuse, Walker Parents Group (1991) (10mins.)
Distributor: Albany Video
This video, with accompanying leaflet, came out of a group-work experience for mothers whose children had been abused.

Although brief, it emphasises the importance of involving non-abusing parents and the wider community in protecting children. Aimed at adults and professionals working with parents.

To a Safer Place, National Film Board of Canada (1987) (58mins.)
Distributor: Educational Media
Documents the journey of an adult survivor as she retraces her childhood through interviewing members of her family, her neighbours, friends and her psychiatrist. All participants are white. It has a very positive message about recovery which can be useful for young people who have experienced sexual abuse. Suitable for adults and teenagers.

Guides for parents and other primary caregivers

Title: *Adopting or Fostering a Sexually Abused Child*
Author: C. Macaskill
Publisher: Batsford Ltd, London
ISBN: 0 7134 6760 6

Title: *Come and Tell Me Right Away*
Author: L. Tschirhart Sanford
Publisher: Ed-U Press, New York
ISBN: 0 934978 12 3

Title: *Helping Your Child be Safe*
Available from King County Rape Relief, 1025 South 3rd Street, Renton, WA 98055, USA. Printed in English, Chinese, Vietnamese, Lao and Cambodian.

Title: *He Told Me Not to Tell*
Available from King County Rape Relief, 1025 South 3rd Street, Renton, WA 98055, USA.

Title: *Mothers of Incest Survivors: Another Side of the Story*
Author: J. Tyler-Johnson
Publisher: Indiana University Press, USA
ISBN: 0 253 20737 1 pbk
      0 25333 096 3 hbk

Title: *No Is Not Enough: Helping Teenagers Avoid Sexual Assault*
Authors: C. Adams, J. Fay and J. Loreen-Martin
Publisher: Impact Publishers, California, USA
ISBN: 0 915166 35 6

Title: *No More Secrets: Protecting Your Child from Sexual Assault*
Authors: C. Adams and J. Fay
Publisher: Impact Publishers, California, USA
ISBN: 0 915166 24 0

Title: *Keeping Safe: A Practical Guide to Talking with Children*
Author: M. Elliott
Publisher: Hodder & Stoughton, London
ISBN: 0 450 43117 7

Title: *Protect Your Child from Sexual Abuse: A Parent's Guide*
Author: J. Hart-Rossi
Publisher: Parenting Press, Seattle, WA, USA
ISBN: 943990 06 8

Title: *The Sexual Abuse of Children*
Author: M. Saphira
Publisher: Papers Inc., Box 47, 398 Ponsonby, Auckland, New Zealand

Title: *Take Care: Preventing Child Sexual Abuse*
Author: C. Corcoran
Publisher: Poolbeg Press, Dublin
ISBN: 1 85371 000 8

Title: *When Your Child has been Molested*
Authors: K. Hagans and J. Case
Publisher: Lexington Books, Lexington, Mass., USA
ISBN: 0 669 17980 9

CHAPTERS TWO AND THREE
Resources for reducing risk and identifying sexual abuse, including primary prevention material

Videotapes
Feeling Yes, Feeling No, National Film Board of Canada (1986) (72mins.)
Distributor: Educational Media Video & Film Ltd, 235 Imperial Drive, Rayners Lane, Harrow, Middlesex HA2 7HE (Tel. 0181–868 1908/1915; Fax 0181–868 1991)
This prevention programme is designed for use in schools with 5-11-year-olds. There are four segments: the first explains the rationale for the programme and summarises the component parts for parents and teachers; the next three segments develop the themes of 'yes' and 'no' feelings, dealing with strangers, and rehearsing telling if you have a problem with touching. It moves gradually to abuse within families. Adults role-play scenes for the children. Most but not all participants are white.

Kids Can Say No, Skippon/NSPCC (1985) (20mins.)
Distributor: Albany Video Distribution, Battersea Studios, Television Centre, Thackeray Road, London SW8 3TW (Tel. 0171–498 6811; Fax 0171–498 1494)
The material is based on the 'Feeling Yes, Feeling No' programme developed in Canada, and designed for use both at home and in the classroom. Four children rehearse what to do if they are touched in ways they do not like. Discussions are led by Rolf Harris. The children are involved in role-play situations with adults. There is one black male child with three white children, a boy and two girls. Aimed at 5-11-year-olds.

Strong Kids, Safe Kids (38mins.)
Distributor: CIC Video, UIP House, 45 Beadon Road, London W6 0ND (Tel. 0181–846 9433)
This is an Anglicised version of an American prevention video, designed for home use, which includes cartoon characters like Yogi Bear and the Smurfs. Various scenarios are presented to

the children and they are encouraged to think how they would respond. The message is primarily about strangers and encourages children to say no, go away; and to tell someone.

Whattado (1984) (16mins.)
Updated as *What to Do about Secrets* (1989) (20mins.)
Distributor: Educational Media

These American videos are aimed at under-5s, and deal with issues of bullying from both children and adults. They use puppets to get the message across about what to do. All participants are white.

You Can Say No, Girls' Video Project (1987) (40mins.)
Distributor: Albany Video

A programme made by young women for young women, this covers a range of abusive situations from harassment to incest and rape. There is a critique of the legal system and comments about how boys and girls are socialised. All participants are white and working-class.

Books for children under 10

Title: *Feeling Happy, Feeling Safe*
Author: M. Elliott
Publisher: Hodder & Stoughton, London
ISBN: 0 340 55386 3

A book which teaches children how to deal with a range of situations from bullying to sexual advances by someone they know.

Title: *I Belong to Me*
Authors: L. Atkinson, L. Kemp-Keller, B. Pawson
Publisher: Whortleberry Books, Kelowna, BC, Canada
ISBN: 0 9691940 0 5

Introduces the topic of good and bad touches to pre-school and primary children. Also discusses what to do if you don't like the touches.

Title: *If You Meet a Stranger*
Author: C. Jessel
Publisher: Walker Books, London
ISBN: 0 7445 1602 1
Real-life characters and photographs are used to teach young children how to take care if they meet a stranger. Aimed at 3-5-year-olds

Title: *It's My Body*
Author: L. Freeman
Publisher: Parenting Press, Seattle, WA, USA
ISBN: 0 943990 03 3
This books goes with the parent guide by Janie Hart-Rossi. It provides children with ideas on how to deal with uncomfortable touches from tickling to sexual abuse.

Title: *It's OK to Say No*
Publisher: Peter Haddock Ltd, Bridlington
ISBN: 0 7105 0389 X (Colouring Book) and 0 7105 0390 3 (Activity Book)
As the title suggests this book tries to identify situations where it is okay to say no to adults.

Title: *Katy's Yucky Problem*
Author: L. Morgan
Publisher: Papers Inc., New Zealand
ISBN: 0 908780 20 6
A story about trusting your feelings and making decisions. It aims to help children decide what to do and who to tell if they are touched in inappropriate ways.

Title: *Mousie*
Author: K. Rouf
Publisher: The Children's Society, London
ISBN: 0 907324 355
A story about a teddy called Mousie, who experiences some bad touching but is able to tell and be protected.

Title: *Mr T's Be Somebody or Be Somebody's Fool*
Authors: Mr T. and P. Elbling
Publisher: W. H. Allen & Co. plc, London
ISBN: 0426 20188 4

A book for black and white children about assertiveness and valuing themselves.

Title: *Private Zone*
Author: F. S. Dayee
Publisher: Warner Books, New York, USA
ISBN: 0 446 38311 2

Outlines good and bad touching and introduces the idea of private parts. Aimed at 3-5-year-olds.

Title: *Rabbit's Golden Rule Book*
Author: M. Twinn
Publisher: Child's Play International Ltd, Swindon
ISBN: 0 85953 298 4

Teaches children about stranger danger.

Title: *Secrets*
Publisher: The National Deaf Children's Society, London
ISBN: 0 904 691 39X

This book has sign-supported English. It is to be used with an adult to explore what to do about secrets including seeing someone break into a car as well as being offered sweets, dealing with bullying and unwanted touching. Specifically designed for young deaf children but may be useful for older deaf children.

Title: *Taking Care with Strangers*
Authors: K. Petty and L. Kopper
Publisher: Franklin Watts, London
ISBN: 0 86313 679 6

Two children, a girl and a boy, are taught about stranger danger.

Title: *The Trouble with Secrets*
Author: K. Johnson
Publisher: Parenting Press, Seattle, WA, USA
ISBN: 0 943 99022 X pbk
     0 943 99023 8 hbk

This book aims to help children decide when to share secrets and when it is all right to keep them.

Title: *You Choose*
Publisher: Keep Deaf Children Safe Project
ISBN: 0 9044691 32 2

This book has been designed for deaf children and includes sign-supported English on each page along with the writing. It explores personal safety and helps introduce the concepts of appropriate and inappropriate activities. The only book of its kind. Keep Deaf Children Safe Project, c/o National Deaf Children's Society, 15/16 Dufferin Street, London EC1Y 8PD (Tel. 0171–250 0123). The KDCS project offers counselling, training and resources for anyone working or living with deaf children.

Title: *We Can Say No*
Authors: D. Pithers and S. Greene
Publisher: Beaver Books, London
ISBN: 0 09 950690 4

Aims to teach children to be assertive and confident, able to cope with the toughest and most confusing situations.

Books for children between 10 and 14

Title: *Bully*
Author: Y. Coppard
Publisher: Bodley Head Children's Books, London
ISBN: 0 370 31524 3

A book about a young girl who is being bullied at school and how she overcomes this.

Title: *Help Yourself to Safety*
Authors: K. Hubbard and E. Berlin
Publisher: The Chas Franklin Press, Edmonds, WA, USA
ISBN: 0 932091 01 6

Offers a range of situations to children about protecting themselves and encourages them to think of what to do.

Title: *No More Secrets For Me: Helping to Safeguard Your Child Against Sexual Abuse*
Author: O. Wachter
Publisher: Penguin, Harmondsworth, Middlesex
ISBN: 0 14 009287 0

Four stories about different situations where children are in unsafe situations – from approaches by strangers to sexual advances by a family member.

Title: *Secrets* (black family version)
Author: K. Rouf
Publisher: The Children's Society, London
ISBN: 0 907324 38X

This and the following version, written by a young survivor of sexual abuse, describe how difficult it is to tell. Describes the young person's feelings and confusion very clearly.

Title: *Secrets* (white family version)
Author: K. Rouf
Publisher: The Children's Society, London
ISBN: 0 907324 371

Title: *A Very Touching Book*
Author: J. Hindman
Publisher: McClure-Hindman Associates, Oregon, USA
ISBN: 0 9611034 1 8

A book about different kinds of touching.

Title: *Willow Street Kids*
Author: M. Elliott
Publisher: Pan/Piccolo Picture Books, London
ISBN: 0 233 97954 9

A series of stories to help children find ways to keep safe. Covers a spectrum of situations from bullying to unwanted sexual advances from a known adult.

Books for teenagers on keeping safe

Title: *Safe, Strong and Streetwise*
Author: H. Benedict
Publisher: Lightning
ISBN: 0 340 48495 0

Adapted from the United States, a useful resource book dealing with issues of personal protection for adolescents.

Title: *Too Close Encounters and What to Do about Them*
Author: R. Stones
Publisher: Piccadilly Press, London
ISBN: 0 946826 69 2

Practical advice on dealing with unwanted sexual encounters.

Title: *Top Secret: Sexual Assault Information for Teenagers Only*
Authors: J. Fay and B. J. Flerchinger
Publisher: King County Rape Relief, Renton, WA, USA
ISBN: 0 941816 20 6

An accessible booklet on sexual assault, dealing with stranger assaults, acquaintance rape and incest. There are quizzes and points for discussion throughout.

Activity books including pictures to colour, quizzes and puzzles that focus on keeping safe or helping children to express their feelings

Title: *The Anti-Colouring Book*
Authors: S. Striker and E. Kimmel
Publisher: Hippo Books, Scholastic Publications, London
ISBN: 0 590 70011 1

Presents a series of imaginary situations and encourages children to draw a picture to go with them.

Title: *Feel Safe*
Author: M. A. Cohen
Publisher: Western Publishing Co. Inc., Racine, WA, USA
ISBN: 0 307 02235 8

Good and bad touches clearly represented. Lots of stickers included and spaces for children to do their own pictures.

Title: *Got to Be Me*
Author: M. Harmin
Publisher: Argus Communications
ISBN: 0 913592 80 3
This book for children aged 5–8 provides a range of imaginary situations and encourages children to fill in the blanks.

Title: *This Is Me*
Author: M. Harmin
Publisher: Argus Communications
ISBN: 0 89505 019 6
This book for children aged 7–9 provides a range of imaginary situations and encourages children to fill in the blanks.

Title: *Greater Expectations*
Authors: T. Szirom and S. Dyson
Publisher: Learning Development Aids, Wisbech, Cambridgeshire
ISBN: 0 90511 4191
A sourcebook for working with girls and young women to build self-esteem.

Title: *Learning to be Strong: Developing Assertiveness with Young Children*
Author: Pen Green Family Centre
Publisher: Changing Perspectives, Northwich
ISBN: 1 872030 02 5
Developed by staff in a family centre for use with staff, parents and children.

Title: *Liking Myself*
Author: P. Palmer
Publisher: Impact Publishers, California, USA
ISBN: 0 915166 41 0
Assertiveness training for children. Encourages children to develop a strong sense of themselves and their rights in an appropriately assertive way.

Title: *The Mouse, the Monster and Me*
Author: P. Palmer
Publisher: Impact Publishers, California, USA
ISBN: 0 915 166 43 7
As above.

Title: *My Book, My Body*
Authors: A. Peake and K. Rouf
Publisher: The Children's Society, London
ISBN: 0 907324 363
Trigger pictures and phrases regarding personal space and feelings that encourage children to complete the sentence and draw their own picture.

Health education material including books about sex education

Title: *The Body Book*
Author: C. Rayner
Publisher: Piccolo Picture Books, London
ISBN: 0 330 25807 9
A simple and clear guide to how the body works, with drawings. A video of the book is available from Video Arts, 68 Oxford Street, London W1N 9LA (Tel. 0171–637 7288). For children under 12.

Title: *The Getting Better Book*
Author: C. Rayner
Publisher: Piccolo Picture Books, London
ISBN: 0 330 29358 3
Covers general issues about bodies and how they deal with childhood bumps and scrapes. For ages 4–11.

Title: *Have You Started Yet?*
Author: R. Thomson
Publisher: Piccolo Picture Books, London
ISBN: 0 330 216 34 7
A book for teenagers about periods.

Title: *Janine and the New Baby*
Author: L. Thomas
Publisher: Little Mammoth, London
ISBN: 0 7497 0651 1

Parents provide answers to their daughter's questions about babies. The family is black. For all children aged 3–6.

Title: *Knowing Me, Knowing You: Strategies for Sex Education in the Primary School*
Authors: P. Sanders and L. Swinden
Publisher: Learning Development Aids, Wisbech, Cambridgeshire
ISBN: 185503 0713

Like the *Taught, Not Caught* book (see below), a valuable resource including a wide range of materials across a number of issues to do with self-awareness and the development of a positive sexual identity. A parents' guide is to be published shortly.

Title: *Loving Encounters: A Young Person's Guide to Sex*
Author: R. Stones
Publisher: HarperCollins, London
ISBN: 0 00 673247X

Deals with puberty and the move towards sharing sexual intimacy emphasising the emotional maturity and sense of responsibility required. For young people aged 12+.

Title: *The Playbook for Kids About Sex*
Author: J. Blank
Publisher: Sheba Feminist Publishers, London
ISBN: 0 907179 16 9

Very explicit and covers areas such as masturbation and sexual orientation which many other books avoid. Can be useful for children who have become very sexualised as a consequence of sexual abuse.

Title: *The Sex Education Dictionary*
Author: G. Mullinar
Publisher: Learning Development Aids, Wisbech, Cambridgeshire
ISBN: 185503 1388

A reference book for young people aged 12+ which contains definitions on sexual and human development, personal relationships, pregnancy and birth.

Title: *Streetwise Youth Rights Comics No. 7*
Publisher: Maxwell Printing, Australia
ISBN: 0815 0486
Clear and accessible comics covering issues of relevance for young people. This issue deals with a number of different topics including AIDS, periods, drugs, and child sexual abuse.

Title: *Taught Not Caught: Strategies for Sex Education*
Author: The Clarity Collective
Publisher: Learning Development Aids, Wisbech, Cambridgeshire
ISBN: 0 905 114 159
A valuable resource book with many exercises and suggestions for tackling a wide range of sex education issues including unwanted sexual touching. For young people aged 12+.

Title: *What's Happening to Me?*
Author: P. Mayle
Publisher: Macmillan London Ltd
ISBN: 0 33033 1124
Deals with puberty and the physical changes. For children under 12.

Title: *Where Did I Come From?: The Facts of Life without Any Nonsense*
Author: P. Mayle
Publisher: Macmillan London Ltd
ISBN: 0 333 24178 9
For children under 12.

Section 2: Facilitating recovery
The resources listed in this section all deal with children who have been sexually abused and who are trying to come to terms with that experience.

For younger children it is helpful to read the book with them. It is useful to have read some of the books for older children and adolescents as well. If you are choosing a book to give to a young person, you will want one which gives a positive message that survival and recovery are possible.

Videotapes
Good Things Can Still Happen, National Film Board of Canada (1992) (21mins.)
Distributor: Educational Media
Aimed primarily at professionals helping children aged 5–12 to recover from an experience of sexual abuse. It is an interactive package which encourages children to participate in the discussions they are seeing between two children, a girl and a boy.

To a Safer Place
Described earlier (see page 161). Can also be useful in explaining the healing process to adolescents.

Books for children under 10
Title: *Daniel and His Therapist*
Author: L. Morgan
Publisher: Papers Inc., New Zealand
ISBN: 0 908780 21 4
Describes some of the consequences for a young boy who was sexually abused by his mother's partner, and how his counselling helps him recover and learn to manage his feelings. For children aged 4–8.

Title: *It's Not Your Fault*
Author: J. A. Jance
Publisher: The Chas Franklin Press, Edmonds, WA, USA
ISBN: 0 932091 03 2
The story of a young girl sexually abused by her step-grandfather, and how she is helped to recover from the experience through the belief and support of those around her. For children aged 8–10.

Title: *Something Happened to Me*
Author: P. Sweet
Publisher: Mother Courage Press, Racine, WA, USA
ISBN: 0 941300 00 5
Different children, both black and white, talk about their feelings about being touched inappropriately and the help they are getting to recover.

Books for children between 10 and 14

Title: *Look Back, Stride Forward*
Authors: M. Saphira and L. McIntyre
Publisher: Papers Inc., New Zealand
ISBN: 0 908780 06 0
Deals with all aspects of abuse – physical, emotional and sexual – and tries to promote understanding and appropriate use of friends for support.

Title: *Megan's Secret*
Author: L. Morgan
Publisher: Papers Inc., New Zealand
ISBN: 0 908780 35 4
A story about a young girl who has been sexually abused and wants to talk about her experience. Includes reactions from friends and family and the help she receives from her counsellor.

Title: *Too Close for Comfort*
Authors: J. Hayward and D. Carlyle
Publisher: Learning Development Aids, Wisbech, Cambridgeshire
ISBN: 1 85503 074 8
For teenagers who have been sexually assaulted within their families. All the stories have a 'twist-a-plot', which means the endings change depending on what is chosen by the reader at key points in the story.

Books for adolescents and adults

Title: *Back in the First Person*
Author: K. Page
Publisher: Virago Press, London
ISBN: 0 86068 642 6

This novel describes the experience of a young woman who is raped by an acquaintance and her struggle to deal with it.

Title: *Black Girls Speak Out*
Authors: Khadj and Charmaine
Publisher: The Children's Society, London
ISBN: 0 907324 60 6
Two young black women write about their experience of contradictory feelings following sexual abuse.

Title: *The Color Purple*
Author: A. Walker
Publisher: The Women's Press, London
ISBN: 0 7043 3905 6
A powerful fictional account of a young black woman surviving physical and sexual abuse through the support of friends and family.

Title: *Crossing the Boundaries: Black Women Survive Incest*
Author: M. Wilson
Publisher: Virago Press, London
ISBN: 1 85381 429 6
A combination of personal testimony and critical analysis for black survivors of sexual abuse, with a detailed resources section.

Title: *Cry Hard and Swim*
Author: J. North
Publisher: Virago Press, London
ISBN: 0 86068 813 5
An autobiographical account of an adult survivor's recovery work. Recounts not only her sexual abuse experience but her work in therapy and the therapeutic process.

Title: *Don't: A Woman's Word*
Author: E. Danica
Publisher: The Women's Press, London
ISBN: 0 7043 4194 8
An adult survivor's story written in diary form.

Title: *Don't Tell Your Mother*
Author: T. Hart
Publisher: Quartet Books, London
ISBN: 0 7043 33772 4

This novel explores the experience of one family struggling to come to terms with sexual abuse. It includes the unsupportive reactions of others and the negative impact this has on the healing process.

Title: *Into Pandora's Box*
Author: K. Rouf
Publisher: The Children's Society, London
ISBN: 0 907324 568

A collection of poems by a young Asian woman detailing her feelings about her experience of sexual abuse.

Title: *I Know Why the Caged Bird Sings*
Author: M. Angelou
Publisher: Virago Press, London
ISBN: 0 86068 511X

An autobiographical account of sexual abuse and its consequences by an acclaimed black American writer. It is embedded in a lifetime of experiences, putting it into context, and the author clearly writes about her own recovery process.

Title: *If I Should Die Before I Wake*
Author: M. Morris
Publisher: Dell Publishing, New York
ISBN: 0 440 13989 9

A moving and vivid story about a young girl who has been sexually abused by her father, who reminisces about her experience while sitting up one night considering her options.

Title: *Push Me, Pull Me*
Author: S. Chick
Publisher: The Women's Press (Livewire imprint), London
ISBN: 0 7043 4901 9

A novel about a young woman's journey to recovery following her experience of sexual abuse by her mother's new male partner.

Title: *Secrets Not Meant to be Kept*
Author: G. Miklowitz
Publisher: HarperCollins, London
ISBN: 0 00 673223 2

An older sister becomes concerned for her younger sister and together they deal with the consequences of incest. A novel.

Title: *The Unbelonging*
Author: J. Riley
Publisher: The Women's Press, London
ISBN: 0 7043 3959 5

The fictional story of a young black girl who is abused within her family and her struggle to free herself from the situation.

Title: *Voices in the Night Speaking out about Incest*
Authors: T. McNaron and Y. Morgan
Publisher: Cleis Press, San Francisco
ISBN: 0 939416 02 6

A collection of writings, including poetry, by adult women survivors of sexual abuse, both black and white.

Self-help guides for adolescents and adult survivors to help deal with their experience

Title: *The Courage to Heal: A Guide for Women Survivors of Child Sexual Abuse*
Authors: E. Bass and L. Davis
Publisher: Cedar, London
ISBN: 07493 0938 5

Despite the controversy surrounding this book and its supposed connection to False Memory Syndrome, it – and its companion book, *Allies in Healing* – are still among the very best on offer. Don't be put off reading them. The third edition has a new section, 'Honoring the Truth: A Response to the Backlash', that deals with some of the issues raised by the False Memory Syndrome debate.

Title: *Out in the Open: A Guide for Young People Who Have Been Sexually Abused*
Authors: O. Bain and M. Sanders
Publisher: Virago Press, London
ISBN: 1 85381 184X
A useful handbook for recovery for young people who have been sexually abused.

Title: *Outgrowing the Pain*
Author: E. Gil
Publisher: Dell Publishing, New York
ISBN: 0 440 50006 0
For and about adults who were abused as children.

Title: *Surviving Sexual Abuse: A Handbook for Helping Women Challenge Their Past*
Authors: L. Hall and S. Lloyd
Publisher: Falmer, London
ISBN: 0 7507 0153 6

Resource material on using the statutory agencies
Many local authorities publish leaflets outlining their policies regarding child protection. There are also a number of leaflets published in support of The Children Act which outline legal steps that may be taken to protect your child. They can also be obtained from local authorities.

Title: *Child Protection Procedures: What They Mean for Your Family*
Author: C. Atherton
Publisher: Family Rights Group, London
ISBN: 1 871515 033
Available in English, Bengali, Hindi, Urdu and Welsh.

Title: *Children, Parents and the Law*
Author: E. Rudinger
Publisher: The Consumers' Association, London
ISBN: 0 340 37256 7

A good resource book for children and their parents involved in legal matters.

Title: *Working with Sexually Abused Children: A Resource Pack for Professionals*
Authors: A. Peake and K. Rouf
Publisher: The Children's Society, London
ISBN: 0 907 324 39 8
The pack contains three story books, a colouring book, four booklets and eight practice papers. Especially useful for teachers of both primary and secondary schools.

Title: *Children and the Law*
Author: M. Rae
Publisher: Longman, Harlow
ISBN: 0 582 89334 8
A resource book for adolescents that sets out a young person's legal rights and explains how to manage the legal system.

Resources for preparing children for court appearances
The leaflets 'The Child Witness' and 'Being a Witness', by J. Plotnikoff, are available from The Children's Legal Centre. They can be used with older children.

Title: *Susie and the Wise Hedgehog Go to Court*
Author: M. Bray
Publisher: Hawksmere, London
ISBN: 1 854 18 020 7
For children aged 5–8 who may have to go to court.

Title: *Going to Court*
Authors: A. Peake and O. Otway
Publisher: The Children's Society, London
ISBN: 0907324 55X
This booklet explains clearly the court process with two young women's experiences included.

Useful addresses

Head offices for national organisations are usually in London. You could look up the local branch of these organisations in the telephone directory.

Advocacy Services for Children

1 Sickle Street
Manchester M60 2AA
Tel: 0161–839 8442

Barnardos

Tanners Lane
Barkingside
Ilford
Essex IG6 1QG
Tel: 0181–550 8822

Child Abuse Studies Unit

University of North London
62–66 Ladbroke House
Highbury Grove
London N5 2AD
Tel: 0171–607 2789
Offers information, advice and training on all aspects of child abuse.

Childline

General Headquarters
Royal Mail Building
Studd Street
London N1 0QJ
Tel: 0171–239 1000

Children requiring counselling:

FREEPOST 1111
London N1 0BR
Tel: 0800–1111

Children's Legal Centre

20 Compton Terrace
London N1 2UN
Advice: 0171–359 6251
Publications, Sales and Administration: 0171–359 9392

Clinical Psychological Service: Centre of Advancement

Suite 41–43 Melville Court
Croft Street (off Lower Road)
Surrey Quays
London SE8 5DR
Tel: 0171–394 9028
A therapeutic centre committed to meeting the needs of all children and young people, especially those of black and ethnic communities.

Criminal Injuries Compensation Board
Morley House
Holborn Viaduct
London EC1A 2BP
Tel: 0171–936 3476

Family Rights Group
18 Ashwin Street
London E8 3DL
Advice: 0171–249 0008
Enquiries: 0171–923 2628

Information Service on Incest and Child Sexual Abuse
Rasjidah St John
24 Blackheath Rise
London SE13 7PN
Tel: 0181–852 7432

Keep Deaf Children Safe
Project Co-ordinator:
Margaret Kennedy
c/o Nuffield Hearing and Speech Centre
Swinton Street
London WC1X 8BZ
Tel: 0171–837 8855

Kidscape
152 Buckingham Palace Road
London SW1W 9TR
Tel: 0171–730 3300
Fax: 0171–730 7081
Offers training programmes for use in schools to help children

learn about keeping safe by role playing difficult situations and developing coping strategies and the confidence to tell a trusted adult.

Lambeth Women and Children Health Project
Angel Town Estate
8 Hollis House
Overton Road
London SW9 7JN
Tel: 0171 737 7151
A community project which will offer support for non-abusing parents following sexual abuse. Also offers counselling for women who have been sexually abused as children.

The Law Society
113 Chancery Lane
London WC2A 1PL
Tel: 0171–242 1222
Provides information on solicitors who sit on Child Care Panels.

MOSAIC
c/o Barnardos NE Division
The Resource Centre
Orchard House
Fenwick Terrace
Jesmond
Newcastle-upon-Tyne NE2 2JQ
Tel: 0191–281 5024
A service for mothers of

children who have suffered sexual abuse.

National Coalition of Sexual Abuse of Children and Adults with Learning Disabilities
c/o Dr A. Craft
Department of Mental Handicap
University Hospital
Nottingham NG7 2DH

NCH Action for Children
Head Office
Policy & Information Dept
85 Highbury Park
London N5 1UD
Tel: 0171–226 2033
Working towards setting up a national network of sexual abuse treatment centres.
Fourteen projects are already working.

NSPCC
42 Curtain Road
London EC2A 3NH
Tel: 0171–825 2500
Advice and referrals (24 hour):
Linkline 0800–800500
Runs treatment centres for families where abuse (including sexual abuse) is an issue. For local offices consult your telephone directory.

Ombudsman:
If you are unhappy with how your complaint has been dealt with.
Health Services
Church House
Great Smith Street
London SW1P 3BW
Tel: 0171–276 2035

Local Government
21 Queen Anne's Gate
London SW1H 9BU
Tel: 0171–915 3210

Press Complaints Commission
1 Salisbury Square
London EC4Y 8AE
Tel: 0171–353 1248
Helpline: 0171–353 3732

Rape Crisis Centre
Many centres run survivors groups and after-support and advice to mothers of children who have been sexually abused. Check your local telephone directory.

Samaritans
Administrative Office
46 Marshall Street
London W1V 1LR
Tel: 0171–734 2800
Also listed in local telephone directories.

SCOSAC
(Standing Committee on
Sexually Abused Children)
73 St Charles Square
London W10 6EJ
Tel: 0181–960 6376/969 4808
Runs a training and consultancy
service for professionals, as
well as providing information
and resources on many aspects
of sexual abuse. Also runs a free
helpline for professionals called
'Sounding Board'.

National Council for Voluntary Organisations
Regent's Wharf
8 All Saints Street
London N1 9RL
Tel: 0171–713 6161
Contact to obtain a newsletter
called *MASH* (Mutual Aid and
Self-Help). Issue 27 has an
article on self-help groups and
questions that should be asked
before joining specifically in
relation to sexual abuse self-
help groups.

The Survivors' Directory
Broadcasting Support Services
Victoria House
21 Manor Street
Ardwick
Manchester M12 6AD
Tel: 0161–272 7722
Lists a large number of services

throughout the UK. Regularly
updated and available on
subscription for £10 for funded
organisations and £5 for
individuals.

Voice
Bushy Cottage
Grassy Lane
Burnaston
Derby DE6 6LN
Tel: 01332–510 036
A national self-help action
group for young people with
learning disabilities and their
families coping with the issues
surrounding sexual abuse.
Campaigns for legal reforms.

Voices from Care
254 Cowbridge Road East
Cardiff
South Glamorgan CK5 1GZ
Tel: 01222–398 214
Formerly the National
Association of Young People in
Care.

'WHO CARES?' Trust
Citybridge House
Goswell Road
London EC1V 7JD
Tel: 0171–251 3117
Produces a quarterly
publication called *Who Cares?*
for children and young people

aged 10–18 for a £16 annual subscription.

Women's Support Project
1700 London Road
Glasgow G32 8XD
Tel: 0141–554 5669
0141–556 5205 (Qwerty phone)
This is a confidential voluntary organisation that offers support, information and training on all aspects of abuse. They also have a resource library. Services for deaf women and their children have been developed.

Working Group against Racism in Children's Resources
460 Wandsworth Road
London SW8 3LX
Tel: 0171–627 4594
Can provide information on material and resources that cater for the needs of black and minority ethnic children.

NOTES AND REFERENCES

CHAPTER ONE

1. Kelly, L., Regan, L. and Burton, S. (1991), *An Exploratory Study of the Prevalence of Sexual Abuse in a Sample of 16–21-year-olds*, London: Child Abuse Studies Unit.
2. Mental Health Foundation (1993), *Mental Illness: The Fundamental Facts*.
3. Austin, A. (1994), personal communication based on child protection statistics for the London Borough of Tower Hamlets.
4. Prior, V., Lynch, M. and Glaser, D. (1994), *Messages from Children: Children's Evaluations of the Professional Response to Child Sexual Abuse*, NCH Action for Children in partnership with the Newcomen Centre and the Bloomfield Clinic at Guy's Hospital, London.
5. Kelly et al., op. cit.
6. ibid.
7. Finkelhor, D. (1984), 'Four Preconditions: A Model', in *Child Sexual Abuse: New Theory & Research*, London: Collier Macmillan.
8. Morrison, T., Erooga, M. and Beckett, R. (1994), *Sexual Offending Against Children: Assessment and Treatment of Male Abusers*, London: Routledge.
9. ibid.
10. The balance in favour of possible protectors is likely to happen in families and neighbourhoods but in some situations such as residential units it can be in favour of perpetrators. The most recent incident to attract media attention is the systematic physical and sexual abuse of young people in the care of Clwyd County Council in Wales. However, other similar situations have given rise to public inquiries including Leicestershire's Beck Inquiry, Staffordshire's Pindown Report, and the Hughes Report which looked at Kincora in Northern Ireland, to name a few of the most well known.

CHAPTER TWO

1. The use of 'anatomically correct' dolls has been the subject of much debate. Anatomically correct is a misnomer; the dolls, for instance, have no ears. The female genitals have no clitoris. The dolls are no longer used in investigative interviews follow-

ing guidance from the Government on how to interview children (*Memorandum of Good Practice on Video-recorded Interviews with Child Witnesses for Criminal Proceedings* [1992], London: HMSO). The following references are useful in giving an overview of the debate:

Yates, A. and Terr, L. (1988), 'Anatomically Correct Dolls – Should They be Used as the Basis for Expert Testimony?', *Journal of American Academy of Child & Adolescent Psychiatry*, 27(2) 254–7; 27(3) 387–8.

Glaser, D. and Collins, C. (1989), 'The Response of Non-sexually Abused Children to Anatomically Correct Dolls', *Journal of Child Psychology & Psychiatry*, 30, 547–60.

2. Kelly et al., op. cit.
3. DNA testing matches the genetic material of the child against the mother's and putative father's. All of the child's genes come from the parents.
4. Summit, R. (1983), 'The Child Sexual Abuse Accommodation Syndrome', *Child Abuse and Neglect*, 7, 177–94.
5. Oppenheimer, R. et al. (1985), 'Adverse Sexual Experience in Childhood and Clinical Eating Disorders: A Preliminary Description', *Journal of Psychiatric Research*, 19, 357–61.
6. Recent reforms regarding the age of consent for homosexual acts between men lowered the age from 21 to 18 years. There is no age of consent for homosexual acts between women.
7. Droisen, A. (1986), *Crime of Violence* (video), distributed by Glenbuck Films, c/o BFI, 21 Stephen Street, London W1P 1PL (Tel. 071–957 8938).
8. Jacqui Saradjian has researched female sexual offending and is currently writing up her work for publication. Her unpublished research reports are at Leeds University.

CHAPTER THREE

1. Kidscape, 152 Buckingham Palace Road, London SW1W 9TR.
   Feeling Yes, Feeling No programme available from Educational Media Film & Video Ltd, 235 Imperial Drive, Rayners Lane, Harrow, Middlesex HA2 7HE.
   Both of these programmes are designed for use in primary schools.
2. Wurtele, S. and Miller Perrin, C. (1992), *Preventing Child Sexual Abuse: Sharing the Responsibility*, Lincoln, Nebraska, and London: University of Nebraska. This book has very good summaries of the development of sexual awareness in children.

3. *Feeling Yes, Feeling No* (1986) from the National Film Board of Canada.
4. Peake, A. and Smith, G. (1987), unpublished data from girls' group.

CHAPTER FOUR

1. Mothers of Sexually Abused Infants and Children leaflet (1993). Contact through MOSAIC at Barnardos NE Division, Orchard House, Fenwick Terrace, Jesmond, Newcastle-upon-Tyne NE2 2JQ.
2. Liz quoted in an article 'Mother Courage' by Claire Messud in the *Guardian*, 21 April 1993.
3. Hooper, C.A. (1992), *Mothers Surviving Child Sexual Abuse*, London: Routledge.
4. MOSAIC leaflet, op. cit.
5. ibid.
6. Wilson, M. (1993), *Crossing the Boundary*, London: Virago Press.
7. Mars, M. (1989), 'Child Sexual Abuse and Race Issues' in *After Abuse: Papers on Caring for a Child Who Has Been Sexually Abused*, London: British Agencies of Adoption and Fostering. See also *Black Girls Speak Out* by Charmaine and Khadj (1991), London: Children's Society.
8. Nicarthy, G. (edited and adapted by Jane Hutt) (1991), *Getting Free: A Handbook for Women in Abusive Situations.* (British edition), London: Journeyman.

CHAPTER FIVE

1. Summit, R., op. cit.
2. Finkelhor, D. and Browne, A. (1985), 'The Traumatic Impact of CSA: A Conceptualization', *American Journal of Orthopsychiatry*, 55(4), 530–41.
3. ibid.
4. Sgroi, S. (1982), *Handbook of Clinical Intervention in Child Sexual Abuse*, Lexington, Mass.: Lexington Books.
5. Post-traumatic Stress Disorder (PTSD) is an exaggerated but understandable response to a recognisable stressor that can involve unwanted flashbacks to the trauma, often activated by triggers to the memory.
6. The three stranger questions: 'Do I have a yes or no feeling about "x"?' 'Does someone I trust know where I am?' 'Can I get help if I need it?' from the *Feeling Yes, Feeling No* pro-

gramme can be useful. If the answer is no to any question, then the child is advised not to go.

7. Mitra, C. (1987), 'Judicial Discourse in Father–Daughter Incest Appeal Cases', *International Journal of the Sociology of Law*, 15(2), 121–48. See also Yates C. (1990), 'A Family Affair: Sexual Offences, Sentencing and Treatment', *Journal of Child Law*, April/July issue, 70–76.

8. Judge Ian Stanforth Hill made this statement in 1993. In October 1993 he conditionally discharged two men convicted of unlawful sexual intercourse with a 13-year-old girl, saying that she had tried to satisfy her sexual desires, the *Guardian*, 29 July 1994. In the same issue, Judge John Whitely is reported fining a 44-year-old man £50 for sexually assaulting a six-year-old girl.

9. Ryan, G. and Lane, S. (eds) (1991), *Juvenile Sexual Offending – Causes, Consequences and Corrections*, Lexington, Mass.: Lexington Books.

10. Smith, G. (1994), 'Parent, Partner and Protector: Conflicting Role Demands' in Morrison et al., op. cit.

CHAPTER SIX

1. See for example Social Care Association, 'Freedom to Speak: Duty to Care (How to Promote Good Practice and Complain Effectively)' available from *Care Weekly* (Guidelines), 9 White Lion Street, London N1 9XJ.

2. Smith, G. (1992), Thamesmead Girls' Group Evaluation, unpublished report submitted to the London Borough of Greenwich ACPC.

3. ibid.

4. Morrison et al., op. cit.

5. Smith, G., (1992) op. cit.

6. McCormick, K. (1993), 'Questioning Self-Help Groups' in *Mutual Aid and Self-Help: The Self-Help Centre Bulletin*, 27, Spring, 5.

CHAPTER SEVEN

1. Lewis, A (1992), 'The Background to Working in Partnership' in Thoburn, J. (ed), *Participation in Practice – Involving Families in Child Protection*, Norwich: University of East Anglia, 1–5.

2. Smith, G. (1987), 'Recognition of Sexual Abuse: A Clinical Developmental Approach', paper presented to North Tyneside Area Review Committee.

3.   Home Office in conjunction with the Department of Health (1992), *Memorandum of Good Practice on Video-recorded Interviews with Child Witnesses for Criminal Proceedings*, London: HMSO.
4.   The Children Act 1989, S.43, London: HMSO. The Children Act is the major piece of legislation involved in child protection work in civil proceedings.
5.   ibid.
6.   Whilst insurance companies are relaxing their attitudes to HIV testing, at present only two have actually changed the wording on the forms enquiring if applicants have had a positive test result in place of the previous question which asked if a test had been done. Employers and insurance companies can still stigmatise individuals who are HIV positive. Also the child when older may not want to have to discuss the reasons why the test was done in the first place. (Information provided by Ivan Massow Associates.)
7.   The Criminal Justice Act 1988 abolished the need for corroboration and made it possible for children to give evidence in Crown Court through a video link.
8.   The Sexual Offences (Amendment) Act 1976, London: HMSO.
9.   Smith, G. (1992), 'Preparing Children for Criminal Proceedings in Sexual Abuse' in Biggs, V. and Robson, J. (eds) *Developing Your Court Work Skills*, London: BAAF, 42–58.
       Aldridge, J. and Freshwater, K. (1993), 'The Preparation of Child Witnesses', *Journal of Child Law*, 5(1), 25–7.
       See also London Family Court Clinic, Child Witness Project (1991), *Reducing the System-induced Trauma for Child Sexual Abuse Victims through Court Preparation, Assessment and Follow-up: Executive Summary*, 254 Pall Mall Street, Suite 200, London, Ontario, Canada N6A 5PG.
10.   The Children Act 1989.
11.   Eaton, L. (1994), 'Injury Time', *Community Care*, 27 January 1994, 21.

The Women's Press is Britain's leading women's publishing house. Established in 1978, we publish high-quality fiction and non-fiction from outstanding women writers worldwide. Our exciting and diverse list includes literary fiction, detective novels, biography and autobiography, health, women's studies, handbooks, literary criticism, psychology and self help, the arts, our popular Livewire Books for Teenagers young adult series and the bestselling annual *Women Artists Diary* featuring beautiful colour and black-and-white illustrations from the best in contemporary women's art.

If you would like more information about our books, please send an A5 sae for our latest catalogue and complete list to:

The Sales Department
The Women's Press Ltd
34 Great Sutton Street
London EC1V 0DX
Tel: 0171 251 3007
Fax: 0171 608 1938

The Women's Press Handbook Series

Kathy Nairne and Gerrilyn Smith
Dealing with Depression

Second Edition – Fully revised and updated

Why do so many women suffer from depression?
How can we defend ourselves against this common
problem and get out of what can quickly become a
vicious circle?

Kathy Nairne and Gerrilyn Smith, both clinical
psychologists, draw on their extensive professional
experience together with the experiences of a wide
range of women sufferers to offer this down-to-earth
and comprehensive guide. From identifying the
causes of depression to understanding the many
forms it can take, from different ways of coping and
recovering to evaluating the help available, here is an
essential handbook for anyone who has experienced
depression, either in themselves or others.

**'A straightforward, practical guide...it explores its
subject in depth.'** *Company*

**'I can thoroughly recommend this practical,
sympathetic and non-patronising book.'**
London Newspaper Group

Health/Self Help £6.99
ISBN 0 7043 4443 2

The Women's Press Handbook Series

Margaret Doyle
The A-Z of Non-Sexist Language

Bringing today's vocabulary completely up-to-date,
here is a definitive guide to non-sexist language.

With a complete listing of sexist words and their non-
sexist alternatives; vital clarification of common-usage
words – outlining fully why some words are sexist
and others are not; full cross-referencing; and an
easy-to-use A-Z dictionary format, here is an
invaluable handbook for writers, editors, teachers,
speakers and all who care about the words they use.

Reference/Language £6.99
ISBN 0 7043 4430 0

The Women's Press Handbook Series

Marilyn Lawrence
The Anorexic Experience

Third Edition – Fully revised and updated

Why does anorexia afflict so many women and girls?
Why should a bright young woman suddenly drive
herself to starvation?

Marilyn Lawrence, a professional with over ten years'
specialist experience, offers a clear, accessible and
helpful guide to recognising, understanding and
tackling this insidious illness in yourself and others.
From the fallacy of the 'ideal weight' to resolving
the conflicts that can underpin an eating disorder,
The Anorexic Experience also includes a complete
review of the services and treatments currently
available. Fully revised and updated, with vital new
material, this invaluable handbook remains unmatched.

'An absorbing and important book.' *Nursing Times*

Health/Self Help   £6.99
ISBN 0 7043 4441 6